P9-EGB-262
HURON COUNTY LIBRARY
2 008 238859 4
Donald L. MacRae
Kentville,
Nova Scotia.

27-12-'41

THE FLYING BULL
AND OTHER TALES

THE FLYING BULL
AND OTHER TALES

By
WATSON KIRKCONNELL

Drawings by
J. W. McLAREN

1940
OXFORD UNIVERSITY PRESS
LONDON TORONTO NEW YORK

Note: All characters in these tales are purely fictitious.

To

SIR CHARLES G. D. ROBERTS
THE NESTOR OF OUR
CANADIAN LITERATURE

CONTENTS

THE FLYING BULL
AND OTHER TALES

The Drover's Tale *of* THE FLYING BULL

PROLOGUE

Caught by the blizzard, as it fell,
In that old Manitou hotel,
We sat and smoked around the fire,
Watching the birch-wood flames leap higher,
And told tall yarns to while away
The dull, interminable day.
We were a miscellaneous lot
Who thronged that parlour, wide and warm,
And deemed the place a pleasant spot
On such a stressful day of storm,
When all the roads were drifted high
And even trains had ceased to ply.
We were a dozen at the least:
A cattle drover, and a priest,
Two farmers, and a country teacher,
A Lutheran Icelandic preacher,
The driver of the Grey Goose bus
(Whose stoppage caused uncommon fuss),
Two Mounties (both extremely tall,
A Sergeant and a Corporal),
A wholesale "drummer", pale and wan,
And I, a bashful college don.

Still others drifted in and out
From the small village round about,
For work that day was standing still
And they, like us, had time to kill.
There was a merchant, sleek and fat,
Likewise a lawyer, thin and seedy,
A doctor with a red cravat,
A clerk whose voice was high and reedy;
A butcher reared on brewers' nectar,
And a lean, wrinkled school-inspector,
While keeping all our talk in motion
With breezy jest and fertile notion
Was the hotel-man, Michael Casey,
A big, stout fellow, free and racy,
Whose native Irish *savoir faire*
Had freshened in our Western air
Into a bluff and hearty way
That made his guests delight to stay.

He and the drover had been cronies
For many a year in Winnipeg;
Together they had played the ponies;
Each loved to pull the other's leg;
And each in his own virile fashion
Could tell a tale of manly passion.
So, as with breakfast done we sat
About the fire in quiet chat,
He hailed the drover with conviction
And tried to stir him up to fiction:

"Patrick," he said, "you're much the least
Of all men living given to lying.
Tell us the truth about yon beast,
The Angus bull that took to flying!"
  The drover dusted off his vest,
And spat, and gave his pipe a pull,
And then began with quiet zest
His story of the Angus bull:

THE DROVER'S TALE

I

THE toughest bull I ever saw
Was on a farm near Neepawa,
Where an old cowhand, Dave MacMeans,
Kept a big herd of Aberdeens.
Dave was a rough and wrinkled Scot,
With bulbous nose and sunset whiskers;
He liked his whiskey neat and hot—
When young he'd frisked among the friskers.
And sixty years had left him cursed
With stomach ulcers and a thirst.
Two things he'd loved in life's long battle:
Theology and Angus cattle.
And while the Calvinist in him
Waxed fervent on predestination,

He'd argue long with equal vim
That black bulls were the farm's salvation.
  The pride of his own dusky herd
Was 'Mumbo-Jumbo', bull supreme—
The biggest, grimmest, blackest-furred
Of all the brutes of Pharaoh's dream.
He was as black as Satan's dam,
And nigh as tall as Pilot Mound;
The rumblings of his diaphragm
Made thunder thirty miles around;
His ribs were like a Roman arch;
His back was level as the prairie;
His massive legs in stately march
Made a small earthquake through the dairy;
But of his eyes no words can tell—
Within them glowed the fires of hell,
Two lamps of livid yellow, lit
With anger from the nether Pit,
His cows had always found him kind,
But hatred smouldered in his mind
For all our human jacks and queens
Except his master, Dave MacMeans.
Yes, Dave he loved, beyond a doubt,
For the old sanctimonious sinner
Would often give his mammoth snout
A snort of whiskey after dinner;
And so a spirituous bond
Kept beast and man uncommon fond.

II

Now in the spring of '35
David was gathered to his fathers.
On Sunday he had been alive;
On Monday, fierce internal pothers
Brought on that final, fatal quiver
That ends cirrhosis of the liver;
And so by Wednesday night he lay
Dead sober in the graveyard clay.
  Then distant heirs and lawyers, dark as
The vultures at Gehenna's gate,
Came flocking in to share the carcass
Of Dave's unfortunate estate.
Farming they held in cold derision;
So, to facilitate division
And settle up with one clean slash,
They auctioned everything for cash.
One August morning, hot and clear,
A leather-larynx'd auctioneer
Stood in Dave's farm-yard on a table,
Half-way between the house and stable;
And there, amid a throng of buyers,
He bawled the merits of each chattel,
From combines down to common pliers,
And last, not least, Dave's Angus cattle.
The cows and calves were sold with ease
In tempting lots of twos and threes.

('Twas known to every farmer there
How often, at the Winter Fair,
Dave's feeders carried off the Cup,
And with what golden-handed itch
The abattoirs had snapped them up
To grace the banquets of the rich.)
But offers were not plentiful
For Dave's notorious black bull,
Whose most unmitigated choler
Was reckoned dear at half a dollar.
In vain the auctioneer avowed
That any farmer might be proud
To own so vast a thoroughbred,
Most famous in his progeny—
For looking in his eye with dread
Each thought he'd let the monster be.
Just when it seemed the day would end
Without a bid for the old devil,
One quiet voice agreed to spend
A hundred dollars, on the level.
And thus was sold the brute unruly
To Deacon Williams of Plum Coulee,
A man as good as he was strong
And pious as the day is long.
But when at last each buyer sought
To drive away what he had bought,
A streak of dark satanic strife
In Mumbo-Jumbo came to life.

Perchance he blamed on all these men
The loss of his beloved master.
Perhaps there came into his ken
Some dim foreboding of disaster,
Or some distaste for dreary travel
By prairie trail or highway gravel,
Far from familiar scenes to stay,
Southeast, a hundred miles away.
Whatever maggot in the brain
Stirred him to frenzies of disdain,
He pawed the ground, he snorted fire,
And one could see him in his ire
Fiercely and visibly determine
To rid the farm of human vermin.
Straight at the human throng he charged,
Straight at these puny things of shame;
And frantic lanes of fear enlarged
To leave him passage as he came.
Over the fences did they leap
Grasshopper-like by tens and scores;
Shunning the bull's destructive sweep,
Awed by the bull's appalling roars.
Against such cars as had been left
Within the yard he turned his spite,
Venting on them his two-ton heft,
A thunderbolt of Hate and Night.
A dozen Fords were overturned;
He tore the fenders off ten Nashes;

Sparks from his onset lit and burned
A score of Pontiacs to ashes.
When nightfall closed the day's wild session,
It found the bull in full possession.
  But hours later, far from thence,
Good Deacon Williams, sad but trusting,
Invoked the aid of Providence
To give the Devil's bull a dusting:
'Humble his spirit to the earth!
Give me my hundred dollars worth!'
Then with an 'Amen' loud and deep,
In simple faith he turned to sleep.

III

After a night of breathless heat,
There dawned the hottest day that any
Had ever known. Rays seemed to beat
As from a vaster sun; and many
Thought of that final Day of Ire
When all should be destroyed by fire.
The leaves and grasses quickly wilted;
Cracks opened in the baking soil;
On homes that slowly warped and tilted,
The blistering paint began to boil.
Men took to drinking by the keg;
Dumb beasts cried out with moan and mutter;
And thirst-crazed dogs in Winnipeg

Drank melted asphalt from the gutter.
Small wonder was it no one went
On such a day to Dave's old farm
To see the bull's dark discontent
Or seek his frenzy to disarm.
Parched but triumphant, hour by hour,
He stood there in insensate power.
Alone, unchallenged, black as ink,
He scorned to bellow for a drink.

Two hours past the gasping noon,
A dark cloud rose to west-northwest—
Slowly above a world a-swoon
It reared with thunder in its breast,
A roaring, swirling, cloudy funnel,
Black as the entrails of a tunnel.
But though the 'twister' nearer swept,
The Angus bull remained defiant;
Dauntless he stood to intercept
The black, intruding, cloudy Giant.
But all in vain: its mighty force,
Seizing him swiftly from the ground,
Propelled him on a skyward course—
A heavenly bull, southeastward-bound.
And with him went the shattered hulk
Of Dave's best barn, and sped from sight
Revolving round his darker bulk
Like some infernal satellite.

IV

An hour later by the clock,
The storm near Deacon Williams' passed,
So close to all his barns and stock
That the good brother stared aghast.
Then 'mid the tumult of the storm
He saw a black, Satanic form
Swoop down, as though on hidden wings,
And light upon the prairie clay,
While with diminished thunderings
The great tornado ebbed away.
Not fifty yards from Williams' door
There lay a miry open slough.
From it now came a mighty roar.
Out rushed the Deacon, swift to view;
And there, by heck, stood Mumbo-Jumbo,
Up to his belly in the gumbo,
By 'act of God' delivered duly
To his new owner in Plum Coulee.
What thoughts had thronged his heavy mind
During that epoch-making flight
No one can tell; but I'm inclined
To think he got a thorough fright.
For all the rest of his black life
He was most mild—most timid, maybe—
And often Deacon Williams' wife
Would leave that bull to mind the baby."

THE CLERK'S TALE

of

USQUEDUNK, THE FROG-KING

PROLOGUE

"That was a bull," the clerk admitted,
And mused in silence for a space.
"It seems he met with taming fitted
For one of his infernal race.
He brings to mind an old tradition
Told me by Indians, as a child,
About a frog, whose disposition,
Though usually very mild,
Once woke to rage as fierce and full
As would do credit to your bull.
The Netley Marshes were his dwelling,
And there he fought a giant pike.
It is a yarn that's worth the telling:
I'll give the story, if you like."
Around the room entreaties ran,
And so the little clerk began:

I

EIGHT miles due north of Selkirk town,
Great marshes slow the river down
And almost lose its turbid tide
In mazes where its waters glide—
A labyrinth of lakes and channels
And reedy fens and bogs spread forth,
Formed through long geographic annals
By the Red River of the North,
Across whose delta reeds and logs
Now shield a teeming world of life,
Insects and birds and fish and frogs,
In Earth's eternal ways of strife.

Here in the summer twilight rises,
Out of ten million lurking-places,
A living mist that agonizes
Throughout the endless marshy spaces,
Mosquito-hosts that surge and swell
Like choking gases breathed from hell,
An ambient element of voices,
Thin, piercing, and incessant wails—
The song of hatred that rejoices,
The cry of wrath that never fails,
Relentless disembodied tides
That beat against all living things

Like myriad ghosts of parricides,
Fierce vapours formed of unseen wings;
And ever and anon the swarm,
Emerging to material form,
Condenses, as to hellish rain,
In tiny poisoned points of pain.
Yet high above that insect chorus
An utterance more loud, sonorous,
Comes fluting in melodious notes
Out of a million velvet throats,
The descant of the frogs that tread
The marshy delta of the Red.

The master Minstrel of them all
Was Usquedunk, a mighty frog
Whose basso chant at evenfall
Outdid all others in the bog.
Yes, Nature could not boast his fellow,
He was so huge and stout of limb,
And in his hue so bright a yellow
That gold could not compare with him.
His yellow face was mild and placid,
The spots upon his massive back
Might have been etched with nitric acid
Upon a king's memorial plaque.
His thighs were thick and lithe and long,
His toes were tough, his muscles strong;
Yet this gigantic, yellow frog
Was gentle as a pollywog,

For all life's highest joy he found
In ceaseless harmonies of sound,
As if all values life could quote
Were gargled in his golden throat.
A bullfrog, in the sign of *Taurus,*
He deemed it his supreme delight
To lead the wide batrachian chorus
In dulcet flutings to the night.
Loud in the evening there arose
His trills and his arpeggios;
Sometimes he boomed a deep staccato,
A sort of vast and virile shout,
And sometimes sang an obligato
That almost drowned all others out.
True candour would admit, perforce,
His voice was very harsh and hoarse,
And yet it was so deep and loud
That every frog for miles was proud
To hear him every time he spoke
And hail him Emperor of Croak.

II

For years he reigned without dispute
Among the marshes of the Red;
Mudhen and bullfrog, fish and newt,
Acclaimed him as their chosen head;
And every night his ringing voice
Made all the marshy host rejoice.

Only one vicious, wall-eyed pike
Conceived a venomous dislike
For Usquedunk, and vowed, the sinner,
To have the mighty frog for dinner.

One August morning, Usquedunk
Sat calmly on a hemlock trunk,
His favourite throne, beside a pool,
And put his royal brains to school
In fashioning new orchestration
For the sweet-voiced batrachian nation.
Thus waiting for the tune to hatch,
He sat there like a lifeless hummock,
And only stirred at times to scratch
A few mosquitoes off his stomach.
Low in the pool the pike lay hid,
Gauging the distance up the log
To Usquedunk; then nearer slid,
And made a lunge to seize the frog—
But just in time, a flash of grey
Showed the assassin to his prey.
The bullfrog did a high jump, standing,
Giving it all the strength he had,
And made a perfect five-point landing
Upon a nearby lily-pad;
And though his sudden massive weight
Half-sank the leaf and bent it badly,
It still bore up its yellow freight
And saved the vocal monarch gladly.

Alas, the pike, beneath the scene,
Marking the pad's frog-heavy hump,
Rose like a finny submarine
And nipped a morsel off his rump.
The bullfrog gave a roar of pain,
And vaulted to his log again.

III

Each nature has its own reaction.
One might have looked for such as he
To seek melodious distraction
In strains of plaintive elegy,
Lamenting, like a flower in frost,
The tail-piece that he'd loved and lost.
But sudden anger, hot and harsh,
Gripped the great frog of Netley Marsh
And galvanized his mighty frame
Into a leaping yellow flame.
What right had any voiceless fish,
A mute, malicious, mud-brained pike,
To seek to make a breakfast dish
Of him, the Monarch? Thus to strike
Out of the depths without a warning
On such a perfect August morning?
His bosom heaved. His eyes turned black.
He tensed his muscles for attack.
Then like an arrow from a bow
He dove and swam to find his foe,

Who, unsuspecting such intent,
Was idling, slow and insolent.
Three times around the startled fish
A yellow vortex madly raced,—
A streak of frenzied frog a-swish,
A meteor of hate and haste.
Then, with a lamprey's grip, he seized
The breast-fins with his angry jaws;
His front feet round the fins were squeezed;
While farther back his hind-foot claws,
Worked by the pistons of his hips,
Tore the soft belly into strips.
In vain the pike in anguish churned
The water in a burst of power;
In vain in mighty curves he turned
In spurts of eighty miles an hour;
The yellow bullfrog kept his hold
With jaws and hands, and still he tore
The pike's flesh with his toes of gold
And dyed the marshes with his gore,
Until at length, eviscerated
From stem to stern by such attack,
The carcass of the foe he hated
Lay floating lifeless on its back;
And with disdainful strokes the frog
Swam proudly to his hemlock log.

IV

Then the great Monarch, Usquedunk,
Sat long in fervent meditation
Upon that high, familiar trunk,
Until his simmering jubilation
Boiled over in triumphant song
Proclaimed in accents hoarse and strong.
'I've won!' he croaked. 'My foe is sunk!
I've won! I've won! The pike is junk!
So perish all who steal a chunk
From off the rump of Usquedunk!
Chunk o' rump, chunk o' rump, chunk o' rump!' "

THE DOCTOR'S TALE

of

THE CAPTAIN'S CAT

PROLOGUE

Our host threw on another log;
Sparks from the hearth in crackling higher
Roused the young doctor's spotted dog
That dozed beside him near the fire.
"Down, Marmaduke!" the young man said.
"That's a grand name," said Casey, smiling.
"I took it from a cat now dead,"
Replied the youth, "and if beguiling
The hours with most surprising tales
Of bulls and bears and moose and whales
Beside the hearth is your design,
Perhaps you'll lend an ear to mine—
The wildest, weirdest yarn, I'd say,
That ever came from Hudson Bay,
Although no region on this earth
Brings more uncanny tales to birth."
"Tell us your tale," we urged in chorus.
"Tell us," the drover cried, and spat.
And so the doctor laid before us
His story of the Captain's cat.

I

VASTER than Caspian or Black,
Bering or Red or Caribbean,
Or where Okhotsk with storm-lashed back
Chafes at its barriers cyclopean,
Hemm'd by our shores there stretches forth
That *mare nostrum* of the North,
Mediterranean but cold,
Which Manitoba's coasts enfold
And bleak Ungava, white with snow,
And tundras of Ontario,
While to the north its path is spanned
By glacier-fjords of Baffin Land—
A wan and eerie inland ocean
Of which the world has little notion,
Leaving to tracts thus far asunder
Its width and wealth and wizard wonder.
Perhaps a century may come
When many a proud emporium
By Churchill, Nelson, Fish and Moose
Shall garner for Canadian use
The sea-borne riches of the world
Beneath Auroral Flags unfurled,
While coastal cities glitter bright
Far through the chill subarctic night;

Yet even now the great ships ply
Old Hudson's waters without fear,
Braving the grey subarctic sky
To bring Old Europe yet more near
By straits where in the Vikings' day
The gulf of primal chaos lay.
On such a steamship once I went,
A student with a load of steers,
To seek that far-off Continent—
A job Canadians of my years
By thousands gaily undertake
For fun and the adventure's sake.
The fun is always problematic.
It may be rough. And who would care
To be a nurse-maid acrobatic
To cattle down with *mal de mer*?
But we were lucky. Not a breeze
Troubled a sky serene and cool
Across three thousand miles of seas
From Churchill clear to Liverpool.
But memory's pangs will never lack
The luck that struck us coming back.
Yes, for a time, it seemed that Hell
Was playing funeral odes in 'Largo'
For all aboard the *Nancy Belle*
And all the cook-stoves of her cargo.
But first of all I must rehearse
How we incurred a sort of curse.

II

The captain of our sooty craft
Was Jock McBride, a Glasgow skipper,
A dour old man, a trifle daft,
But strict as Pole-star to the Dipper
In all the rules of navigation
That did not need imagination.
No wife had this dull autocrat;
The only living thing he cared for
Was his black-pelted, one-eyed cat,
A beast that pillows were prepared for
And extra mice in cages kept
In quarters where the Captain slept.
I am not squeamish in my ways,
And yet in all my living days
I never felt so strange a quiver
As when that tom-cat gorged on liver;
For he would toss it up and grab it
The way a lynx might rend a rabbit,
And gnaw off chunks and gulp them down
With throaty snarl and evil frown.
Even a vampire might rebuke
The horrid greed of 'Marmaduke'.
  With such a cat and such a captain,
We started back from Liverpool—
Two thousand heavy cook-stoves clapped in
Our vessel's hold. The days were cool,

Even for August, but the sea
Was bright and calm as it could be.
Westbound, we'd passed through Hudson Strait;
Our longitude was eighty-four;
And Cape Southampton stretched in state
To starboard from Coats Island shore;
When suddenly a school of whales
Appeared beside our vessel's rails—
Not the big sperm or cachalot,
But gentle beasts, three fathoms long,
That often haunt that lonely spot,
A kindly, almost human throng,
Suckling their babies in the deep
Or drowsing on the waves asleep.
We slackened speed to watch the sight;
The cat sat on the Captain's shoulder;
I swear his one eye grew more bright
And his rapacious gaze still bolder
Just where a baby whale at rest
Was nuzzling at its mother's breast.
Black Marmaduke let out a mew
Into the Captain's shrivelled ear.
'Eh?' says McBride, 'What's that to you?
You'd like some liver? Ay, that's clear.
I'll not deny you such a trifle.'
And getting out his heavy rifle,
He shot the whale-calf as it suckled,
Then brought the little corpse on board,

And as he ripped it up he chuckled,
Finding fresh liver for the adored
Black-whiskered fiend, old Marmaduke,
By such an unexpected fluke.
But all the crew were not content
To share the Captain's merriment.
The purser was part Eskimo,
Versed in their lore of long ago,
And in a panic he made free
To tell McBride calamity
Would put us all past human aid
Unless atonement should be made.
McBride was wild: 'You silly fool,
I'll put you in the clink to cool
If there is any more such talk.
Off to your bunk, you rascal! Walk!'
And then he turned without a quiver
To stuffing Marmaduke with liver.

III

The baby whale was killed at noon;
All other whales then disappeared;
But on the far horizon soon
To westward rose low clouds that reared
The promise of a bitter gale,
And each was fashioned like a whale—
A phantom whale of wind-blown mist
That towered high with rage, and hissed,

And darkened towards catastrophe
The grey abyss of sky and sea.
'The curse has come,' the purser said;
'In half an hour we'll all be dead!'
And certainly I never saw
Death open half so dark a maw.
Like some black chamber of the deep,
Where two miles down old galleons sleep,
Became that Arctic waste of waters
Through which we ploughed—some pit of slaughters
In which doomed victims gasped for breath
Under the strangling hands of Death.
Then almost as the purser spoke
The swift, tempestuous tumult broke,
And with abrupt, appalling din
A noon-day night rushed roaring in.
Over our reeling bulwarks swept
A frenzied drift of seething foam;
The steamship staggered, swayed, and leapt,
Heading defiantly for home.
But ever slower grew her thrusts
Against the sea's tremendous blows;
Ever more feebly she arose
To face the breakers and the gusts
That wrestled with her horribly
Like some relentless enemy.
Over her decks from stem to stern
A ridge of hissing whiteness poured;

Laden with wreckage did it churn,
And all our boats went overboard.
With bulwarks smashed and flooded deck,
The *Nancy Belle* was half a wreck,
Driving the Captain to conform
And make atonement to the storm.
Out of the pilot-house he stepped,
And with a curse that almost wept,
He took his tom-cat by the tail
And heaved him headlong to the gale.
Like some be-whiskered meteor
Or old King Arthur's hurtling sword,
Shot Marmaduke, and yet he wore
A grin that curdled all on board,
And purred so loud that we could hear it
Above the storm's indignant spirit.
Then out of seas like boiling milk
Rose a black whale and gulped him down,
As if determined thus to bilk
The waves that merely sought to drown.
The tempest ceased. The only stir
Was just a low, Satanic purr,
Deep in the waves, that slowly died
Beneath the fast subsiding tide.

IV

Three mornings later, just at dawn,
We glimpsed the Manitoba coast

Far to the west. The storm had gone
With Marmaduke, but, like a ghost,
Hour after hour, old Jock McBride
Kept gaping from the vessel's side,
Leaving the first and second mate
To mend the steamer's battered state
And steer her on towards Button Bay,
Cape Mercy, and the rocky, grey
Old point where once Fort Prince of Wales
Stood guard above white British sails.
Gone was his wrath; his confidence
Had shattered in an hour intense;
And when we reached the Churchill quay
He solemnly abjured the sea.

He lives not far from Brandon now
With twenty acres and a cow,
Also a wife, and she has brought him
A son, John Solomon, and taught him,
Against his fuddled will, the way
To be a father day by day.
Yet sometimes, by a wayward fluke,
He calls his offspring Marmaduke,
And even, with defiant shiver,
Stuffs the poor youngster full of liver."

The Merchant's Tale
of
THE TRAPPER AND THE BEARS

PROLOGUE

Outside the window howled the storm,
And made the room seem yet more warm.
Then said the drummer: "Days like these
Would make the bears and bison freeze.
Sometimes I think it would be best
To let the Red Man keep the West."
The merchant boomed expostulation:
"This weather is not cold," he said.
"Such climate makes a hardy nation.
Rough weather breeds the thoroughbred.
But I have known such cold as makes
This winter, in comparison,
Seem like a summer at the lakes,
A picnic day for everyone."
Expectant silence greeted this.
"Listen," he cried. "My tale is truth."
And so he told with emphasis
A trapping story of his youth:

I

THE coldest day I ever knew
Was New Year's, back in '22,
Out in the bush near Kapuskasing,
Where, as a trapper, I was facing
The grimmest prospect I had known
Since first I started on my own.
I had no money, to begin with,
And just the clothes upon my back,
Guns, traps, an axe, a knife to skin with,
Four snarling huskies, and a shack.
The spot I'd chosen was the worst
From Porquis Junction west to Hearst—
At least it seemed that way to me
As rations gave out steadily
And in my traps I failed to find
Much paying fur of any kind.
To make things worse, it was my dream
To get some cash, to cease to roam,
To form a matrimonial team,
And have some kids and rear a home,
Back in some thriving little town;
For I was keen to settle down.
Christmas brought neither cheer nor smiles—
The dogs and I were facing hunger

Until I trekked in, thirty miles,
To beg some food. When one is younger,
So piteous a case no doubt
Can blot the sun completely out,
And so, for four days I debated
This course of action that I hated.

Next morning, I was just departing
When heavy weather checked my starting.
The day began with flakes of snow
That fell in droves by half past seven,
Flooding a silent world below
Out of a dark and windless heaven.
They fluttered down, a flood of fleece,
Filling the morning sky completer
Than if ten billion big white geese
Were being plucked by old Saint Peter—
Thus sending, from the sky's high crown,
An avalanche of eiderdown
That soon had mounted, heap on heap,
To a white blanket, four feet deep,
And bent the branches of the spruce
Until it almost snapped them loose.
Towards evening, snowfall slackened off,
But a wild gale then smote the cabin
With shriek and sob and wail and cough
And through each cranny seemed to stab in
With icy daggers of derision,
While through the window-pane my vision

Saw in a maddened maelstrom go
A streaming flux of blinding snow
Torn from the spruce-trees' tossing boughs
And from the ground. In wild carouse,
Earth seemed to shatter, fuse, and fade,
And in white frenzy to disperse,
As if some cosmic Hand had made
A milk-shake of the universe.

II

For six and thirty hours the wind
Raged madly on, and kept me pinned
There in my cabin, where my cupboard,
Like that of well-known Mrs. Hubbard,
Was grimly scant of food to feed
Me and my huskies in our need.
So, when the third day dawned at last
And all the storm was plainly past,
I went outside to find my sled
And mush to town to get some bread.
My little shack was almost hid
Under a mighty drift of white;
Smoke from my chimney upward slid
High in the frosty morning light,
A slender column, pale and wan,
Athwart the sundogs of the dawn;
But I had little time to gaze
On winter's strange and eerie ways.

Giving each husky as a treat
A cast-off moccasin to eat,
I chewed in haste my last cold bannock,
And, with a certain sense of panic,
I started in a hurry, tracing
The shortest trail to Kapuskasing.

A frozen creek off Woman River
Was windswept clear of all its snow.
My lead-dog here stopped, all a-quiver,
And when I tried to make him go,
He scratched the ice and gave a bark
That sounded like a curt remark.
I came to look. The little creek
Had frozen solid in its bed,
And in the ice, not far to seek,
Were six fresh pickerel, frozen dead.
Thus I had chopped, five minutes later,
From this first-class refrigerator,
A savoury dinner for my dogs
And for myself. I split some logs,
Built up a fire and fried a fish
Finer than any king could wish.
But the delay and bitter frost
Persuaded me to stop and camp,
Counting the time as safely lost
In such a long, exhausting tramp.
And so, with sleep my chief desire,
I lay down near the blazing fire.

III

When I awoke, my dogs had vanished,
Leaving no trace that I could see
Beyond the heaving drifts that banished
All thought of stalking them for me.
The fire was out, and nature dealt
Such cold as I have never felt
In all my life, before or since:
It made my aching eyeballs wince,
And seared my anguished lungs and throat
As if some hidden fire smote
My tissues, mingled in my breath,
And doomed me to a gasping death.
My brows and lashes slowly froze,
My cheeks felt cut in tingling strips,
And the slow trickle from my nose
Formed icicles along my lips.
Yet in a crisis so terrific
My first desire was scientific,
An urgent impulse to be sure
About the present temperature.
I should have told you, in digression,
How, as a highly prized possession,
I took with me where'er I went
A very handy instrument—
A Fahrenheit thermometer,
To which I daily would refer.

Nor would I leave it at my shack,
For fear, before I happened back,
Some thirsty, wandering Cree would call
And drain it of its alcohol.
So, now, I quickly got it out,
And looked, and looked—and tried to doubt
My eyes' own evidence, but no!—
It stood at ninety-eight below.

I tried to start a fire, but found
My hands too numb to light a match;
And not an ember on the ground
Remained, on kindling wood to catch.
I shouted for my dogs. Amazed,
I heard no sound of my own voice.
My shouts were mute; and standing dazed,
I felt my one remaining choice
Was to keep moving down the trail
To town before my strength should fail.

I had not gone five hundred feet
Before the cold began to get me.
I could not push on nor retreat:
My faltering snowshoes would not let me.
But just when hope was almost gone
I saw a wisp of breath-steam flow
Out of a fissure in the snow
Where a deep drift had formed upon
A cliff-base that in summer gave
Low access to a shallow cave.

Slipping my snowshoes off, I used them
As frantic implements to dig;
And with a vigour that abused them,
I reached the cave. It was not big,
But body-warmth was waiting there
To save me in my chill despair,
For two fat black bears in a heap
Were gently snoring in their sleep.
They were too drowsy to awake,
For when I snuggled down between them
One merely gave his paws a shake
And one growled slightly. I had seen them
Late in the autumn, by the river,
And never dreamed they would deliver
My body from a frosty fate,
But now, in a most friendly state,
I lay between them on my back
And dreamed about my dogs and shack.
How long I dozed, I cannot tell,
But presently I knew right well
That further warmth my veins caressed,
And found, accounting for the heat,
Some fourteen rabbits on my chest
And two fat beavers at my feet,
While every corner round about
That my dim vision could determine
Was packed with squirrels, plump and stout,
And fox, and lynx, and Arctic ermine.

The most unprecedented weather
Had brought these creatures all together,
A timid, cowering set of friskers,
With frozen toes and frosty whiskers.
Of hate or rage they showed no spark,
But proved as mild in disposition
As if the beasts of Noah's Ark
Had tried an Arctic expedition,
And I, a sort of Gulliver,
Had crashed the berths reserved for fur.
In circumstances such as these,
I was, however, rightly grateful
To beasts that would not let me freeze
And meet a death forlorn and hateful.
The only lingering fear of mine
In that uncanny, beast-filled place
Was lest some thoughtless porcupine
Should make a mattress of my face.
The hours passed by. I must have slept,
Although the air grew still more frigid,
And one by one the beasts that crept
About my frame were growing rigid,
Until at last the bears and I
Alone were left that did not die
Under that furry coverlet
That warded off the winter's threat.

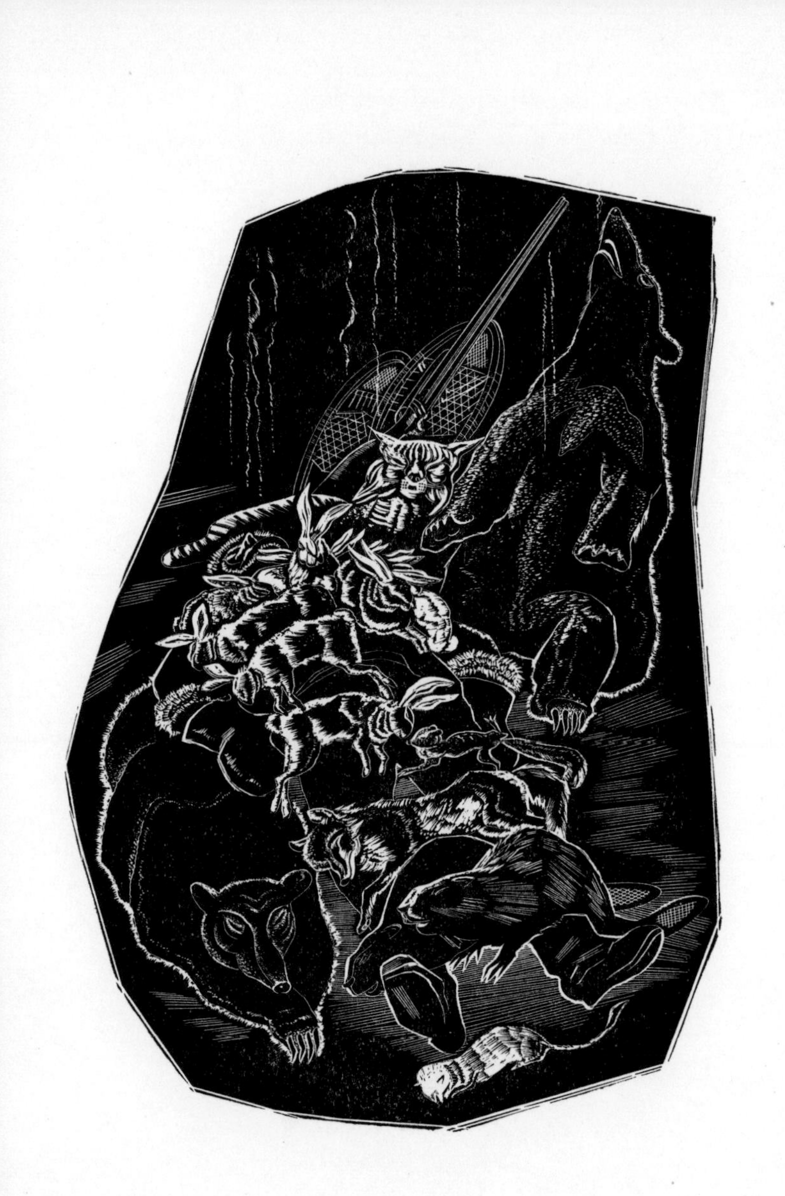

IV

Next day it thawed. I ventured out,
And was surprised to hear a shout
Raised in my own stentorian roar
Where I had called my dogs before.
The cold had chilled my voice, you see,
And left the air-waves all congealed,
And with the rising mercury
My yells thawed out, and as they pealed
Across the snow, before my eyes
I saw my huskies all arise
Out of deep burrows they had dug
To use the snowdrifts as a rug.
I had a busy time that day,
Carting the fur-beasts all away
From that old cave where they had died
While I was on the under side.
I left my friends, the bears, in slumber;
But from the small beasts without number
I got such pelts that, freed from fret,
I cleared two thousand dollars net,
And gave up trapping altogether
Because I didn't like the weather.

All these things happened long ago.
Since then I've wandered to and fro,
And finally have settled down
Here in this quiet little town.

I've married, too, and have acquired
Such children as I long desired:
Five boys and girls, all under ten,
Make me the happiest of men,
With pity for the senseless drone
Who has no offspring of his own.
Yet sometimes, when in January
Cold winds by night sweep off the prairie,
And five small kids, in search of heat,
Come to my bed to warm their feet
On me, their father, I recall
That far-off, coldest day of all.
Then at those little girls and boys
I make a sleepy, bear-like noise,
And urge them (growling hoarse and strange)
To try their mother for a change."

The Drummer's Tale

of

A LATTER-DAY JOB

PROLOGUE

Loudest of all in mourning summer
Among our hearth-side company
Was the glum-eyed, dyspeptic "drummer,"
A sort of sad-faced chimpanzee,
Whose line was wholesale groceries
From custard-powder down to cheese.
He, as a constant traveller,
Faced every winter with demur,
Sadly averse to going places
Across the wind-swept prairie spaces.
"You grouse as loud as Job with boils,"
Said Casey crossly. "Sure it spoils
A social circle, hale and happy,
To see you so depressed and snappy.
Cheer up!"
    "Ay, that I shall," he answered,
"And since you mentioned Job just now,
I shall inform you, true as Hansard,
Of an acquaintance, who, I vow,

Has undergone in Winnipeg
Such woes as poached the Uzzite's egg,
And yet, like him, could take the rap
Without a blink."
"Lead on, old chap!"
Said Casey and we heard intent
A salesman superchanged with slang
Explain in detail what he meant
By citing Job in his harangue:

THE DRUMMER'S TALE

I

IN Manitoba-Uz there dwelt
A grain-man Job, surnamed MacCammon,
Who every day devoutly knelt
Before his god, the mighty Mammon,
Whose temple near the Grain Exchange
Was his delight, for he would range
Along its halls, his grey eyes lit
To serve the Spirit of the Pit.
Job was a perfect man and just,
Kindly and generous in his ways;
And Mammon, for his friendly trust,
Had prospered him throughout his days.
He had a mansion on the Crescent
And a fine cottage at Minaki,

Where his plump wife was effervescent
In summer days, supremely cocky,
Forgetting black-flies, heat, and midges
In cocktail-parties, teas, and bridges,—
While Job, her goose with golden egg,
Was sweating back in Winnipeg.
  A gilded son and heir had he
Who went to University;
And though it vexed him that his son
Had flunked three times in Latin I,
Yet he was made to understand
That social circles of the land
Decreed that beer brought honour high
When drunk with Sigma Alpha Pi.
He had a lively daughter Lou,
Who also parked around the 'U',
And though her grades were rather meagre,
She was a knock-out Junior Leaguer,
Ready to run hotels and stores
And help the world by social chores.
But Job was forthright and old-fashioned:
With him there were no 'ifs' or 'buts';
He kept his rum austerely rationed;
In golf, he always played his putts.
It was his wife who put the skids
Of easy cash beneath the kids.

II

Now Satan, or the Moral Law,
Patrolling Winnipeg one day,
Became aware of Job, and saw
The even tenor of his way;
And, just to test him, turned with glee
To his weak wife and progeny.
Hence was it that a slim, sleek youth,
Hector MacCammon, hot and twenty,
Oblivious to the simple truth
That he had drunk much more than plenty,
Into his father's Lincoln climbed
To drive Lou homeward, cocktail-primed,
From a late dance, where maid and stripling
Had mingled "swing" with open tippling.
Hector was doing sixty-five
When, reaching Osborne Street on Broadway,
A cruiser-car saw him arrive
And plough through red lights. 'That's an odd way,'
Said Sergeant Koyle, 'To drive, bedad!
I think we'll follow up the lad.'

While turning southward on two wheels
On Sherbrook, Lulu grew aware
That the police were at their heels.
And told her brother to take care.
'Phooey!' said Hector. 'Watch me, matey!'
And shoved the Lincoln up to eighty.

The chase was on: and Koyle looked bland
When Hector, with drunk smile seraphic.
At Wolseley swerved up Maryland
Northward against the one-way traffic.
Half on the boulevard he raced,
Nine blocks careening up to Portage;
Of drunken zeal he had no shortage,
For he turned right with dauntless haste
And sought, with automotive roars,
The canyon of the down-town stores.
Just at the Bay, he gave a laugh
And shot south past the Cenotaph;
But Lou let out a maudlin wail,
For Sergeant Koyle was on their tail,
While at his back, ignoring stops,
Came eight fat motor-cycle cops.
Heck swung the Lincoln out of bounds
Across the Legislature grounds
Through flower-bed and grassy ridge,
And headed for the Osborne Bridge.
Just as he reached the narrow way,
A north-bound street-car beat him to it;
The speeding Lincoln could not stay,
But crashed the railing, hurtled through it,
And drowned the screeching son and daughter
Deep in the river's turbid water.
  When their two corpses came home later,
Each face beneath a handkerchief,

Mute sorrow smote their grey-haired pater
But Mrs. Job grew loud in grief:
'I want to be where Hector is!'
She wailed—when suddenly, to please her,
A prompt *angina pectoris*
Stabbed like a knife in Julius Cæsar,
And the plump spirit from her breast
Went gasping forth to be at rest.
Job's troubles were not over yet:
The morning *Free Press,* that next day,
Told how his lawyer, faced with debt,
Had wasted trust-funds quite away,
And all that Job had laid aside
Had gone with the embezzling tide.
Of children, wife, and cash bereft,
Poor Job had very little left,
And was inclined to sit and blub
Down at the Manitoba Club;
Yet no rash word escaped his lips,
Admitting grave paternal slips.

III

There, to bring comfort to his bones,
Came Bildad White and Zophar Jones
And Foster, christened Eliphaz,
Who was a man that loved to razz;
And deep in chairs of padded leather
They talked to Job, discussed the weather,

Till soon all three began to wheeze
Of Job's abrupt calamities.
Quoth Eliphaz: 'It's very sad
To have investments turn out bad.
But it's your fault. I often told you
To watch this pirate who has rolled you.
If you had let me handle things,
Your wealth would not have taken wings.
You were a guy who knew it all,
But you were riding for a fall.'
At the smug phiz of Eliphaz
Job looked in scorn: 'You fool, whereas,
In years, you haven't saved a dollar
Are you the man to raise a holler
About that lawyer, who, it's true,
Was not an all-wise owl like you,
But who, before bad luck began,
Had all the makings of a man?
I'm not the sort that shies at folk—
I'd rather trust them, and be broke.'

Then, with hands clasped on his big paunch,
Bald-headed Bildad turned to launch
A subtle thrust to make Job halt,
And weaken, and confess his fault:
'Your young 'uns would be living still
If you had shown a firmer will;
For when a lad is drunk, I'm thinkin',
You shouldn't let him have the Lincoln.

You spared the rod and spoiled the child:
Just blame yourself if he was wild!'

Job groaned at this, but did not weaken,
And his grim eye shone like a beacon:
'Who would have fancied such a creature
As "Baldy" Bildad turning preacher!
Your wisdom is no gushing fountain.
For you've a son in Stony Mountain,
And daughters out in Hollywood
With reputations far from good.
Come clean! Admit that both our lives
Have been bedevilled by our wives;
For when your own wife won't play ball,
You haven't got a chance at all,
And any hope of discipline
Among your kids is mighty thin.
I really tried to raise my son,
But Mrs. Mac. just let him run.'

A wavering light of triumph broke
In Zophar's eye, and up he spoke:
'If she was silly to the core,
You fool, what did you choose her for?'

'Numskull!' said angry Job to Zophar,
'You've no more gumption than a gopher!
It's plain enough you never married,
And that your heart was never harried—
One minute hot, another frozen.
I didn't choose her. I got chosen!'

IV

Then the three friends of Job were mute,
Because they couldn't faze the brute.
And were provoked, beyond a doubt,
To see, before the year was out,
A buxom widow, named Malvena,
Come as a *deus ex machina,*
And take her place, without ado,
As Job's fair consort Number Two.
She set him up with cash in scads
And seven step-sons, all good lads,
As nest-eggs for a family
That soon had daughters, one, two, three.
Thus his last state was far more blest
Than any other in the West.
And as a tribute to the spectre
Of his lost lad, the errant Hector,
He founded, named for that dull son,
A scholarship in Latin I,
Which his bright step-sons in succession
Win in industrious progression."

THE SERGEANT'S TALE

of

THE MANITOBA STONEHENGE

PROLOGUE

The tightest-lipped of all who sat
Beside that fire and smoked in peace
Was that steel-jawed aristocrat,
The red-coat Sergeant of Police;
So Casey led our talk about,
And tried to draw the Sergeant out.
"I've often heard it claimed," he said,
"That in the West, since Time began
And Adam's kids began to spread,
The Mounties always got their man.
Is it the truth the spalpeens speak,
Or are their facts a trifle weak?"—
Like sunrise on a foggy cliff,
The glimmer of a smile awoke
Behind the Sergeant's mighty whiff
Of eddying tobacco-smoke:
"You say the Force is never wrong;
But though the Law's red arm is long,

And though few men escape our hand
From Morden north to Baffin Land,
Yet there are cases, I'll admit,
That buffalo the boys a bit.
Sometimes sheer luck—or Providence—
Is all that cleans up an offence,
And credit for a crime's solution
Comes from uncanny retribution
That overtakes the wicked, when
They think their crime unseen by men.
I call to mind a baffling case
Up in the northern mining region,
Back in those first prospecting days
Just before Flin Flon brought a legion
Of hard-boiled, strong-arm miners in
To curse the wilderness with din.
Except for Fate, I question whether
The Force had not been bound to fail;
For later, piecing things together,
We got a most amazing tale
From the last member of the gang,
Who died too soon for us to hang."
The Sergeant halted. No one stirred
While he lit up a fresh cigar
And went on, weighing every word,
To tell how, up in wilds afar,
A higher Vengeance came to show
The murder of a sourdough:

I

UP where the line of travel crosses
From Footprint Lake to Nistowasis,
Two hundred miles from Norway House,
Northward by portage-trail and river,
Where Arctic foxes prowl for grouse,
And where the mossy muskegs quiver
By moose-ponds lying cool and black
Through endless spruce and tamarack,
The wealth of milky reefs of quartz,
Ribbing the wilderness of granite,
Now brings prospectors of all sorts
Who hope for gold and come to scan it.
Twelve years ago, before the rush,
Three sourdoughs, one summer day,
Came by canoe, their brows a-flush
With hope that fortune might repay
Their present toil a hundredfold
With rich discoveries of gold.
Bill Smith, Jack Lloyd, and Pete MacLeod,
These unkempt, bearded sons of Chance,
Had left The Pas beneath a cloud
Of most suspicious circumstance
And fogs of dark unproven blame
Arising from a poker game.

Deserved or not, bad fortune dogged them:
A storm on Lake Athapapusko
Upset their boat, and muskeg bogged them
Along a trail near Lake Wekusko;
Most of their grub-stake thus was gone,
But still they struggled grimly on,
Hoping to reimburse their losses
By striking gold near Nistowasis.
Fly-time was at its very worst:
Out of dank woods and bogs accurst,
Blood-hungry blackflies came to fare
Behind their ears and in their hair,
While yellow-banded moose-flies bit,
Raising red welts where'er they lit,
And thick mosquito-clouds would drone
A maddening, murderous monotone.

But blood-gorged pests and rations' shortage
Were for a moment quite forgot
When the men sighted at a portage
A big bull-moose, a perfect shot.
Pete raised his rifle silently,
But the mere movement stirred the bull
To turn for flight past rock and tree,
Just as his finger crooked to pull.
The rifle barked. The great beast lurched,
Then lumbered off.—'I've hit the brute!
Come on!'—And eagerly they searched
Through jack-pine thickets, where his route

Lay clear in hoof-prints in the mud
With broken twigs and flecks of blood.
Then, on a sudden rocky slope,
They found the moose, whose blood's dark streams
Dabbled the quartz-reef of their hope,
The golden out-crop of their dreams!
Ten rods to left and right it spread—
That broad, white vein with gold encrusted—
And the great beast there, lying dead,
Was naught to this, for which they lusted
With all the raw, primeval greed
Of gamblers in their time of need.
Kneeling there, joyous beyond measure,
They gloated on their new-found treasure.

II

Two evenings later found them camped
Far back upon the homeward trail.
By portage short-cuts they had tramped
With their canoe, intent to scale
The brief, abrupt, basalt divide
Out to the Nelson River side
And with all haste record their names,
In Winnipeg, to clinch their claims.
At night-fall, glad to break their trudge,
They camped, and sheltered by a smudge
From ravenous mosquito-hosts,
They ate fried moose and made their boasts

How they would live at highest pitch
Of revelry when they were rich.
Then, by ill fortune, Pete MacLeod
Took from his battered dunnage-pack
A crock of whiskey, and he vowed
He wouldn't wait till he got back:
'Now is the time for celebration!
I am so dry, I know right well
I'd face the Devil and damnation,
Just for a drink!' And all three fell
To boozing in a noisy choir
Around their murky little fire.
Then, as the fumes of whiskey mounted
Up from the belly to the brains,
Drunk Jack to drunken Bill recounted
How much more rich would be their gains
If they should stab drunk Peter through
And share the mine between the two.
'Listen,' he whispered to his mate,
'Get out your skinning-knife, and wait;
And while he snores beside his pack,
We'll stab the rascal in the back.'

Such was their deed, but hands unsteady
Wounded but did not kill their man.
Up leapt poor Pete, half slain already
By streaming wounds, and staggering, ran
Along a little forest-path,
While after him, in drunken wrath,

His comrades, each with dripping knife,
Came lurching on to take his life.

III

Wan moonlight lit the path they took;
And haggard Pete in hopeless terror
Soon slackened pace, with knees that shook,
For he had stumbled in his error
Into the wierdest rocky glen
E'er gazed upon by mortal men.

Hemmed in by high, sheer walls of black,
Steep as the ramparts of a crater,
A treeless rocky pit stretched back,
Shaped like a grave but vastly greater,
And on its phosphorescent floor
Some human tribe of ages gone
Had ranged huge boulders by the score
To form a giant skeleton—
A Manitoba Stonehenge, set
With symbolism grimmer yet.

Into that pit, Pete sickly gazed.
The butchering pair were close behind him,
And on he staggered, horror-crazed:
Down in that gulch they might not find him.
But soon he sank upon the stones
Beside those vast, symbolic bones,
Exhausted, and with swimming eyes
Looked at his slaughterous allies.

'Dead men,' said Bill, 'are slow to quote,
Especially after due cremation.'—
And drew his knife across Pete's throat
With murderous deliberation.
'Now let us build a fire,' he said.
'The blasted gulch is off the trail.
We'll burn this rascal who is dead,
And not a trace will tell his tale.
When we get back to Winnipeg,
We'll say he drowned in Fiddle Lake;
And not a person there will beg
For further details for his sake.'
Under the wan, uncanny moon
They dragged down wood into the chasm;
Pete crackled on his pyre soon,
But Jack Lloyd almost took a spasm
When by the light of that foul fire
A tall, dark stranger seemed to stand
Among the stones beside the pyre
And hail them with uplifted hand.
He looked like some old Indian priest,
But towered nine feet high at least;
And when he spoke, his accents fell
Like organ-music played in hell:
'Do not expect,' he said to Bill,
'To go unpunished for your crime.
Though human law prove not your ill,
Yet rest assured that in due time

You, who have merited such blame,
Shall perish here in penal flame;
And your ally shall earn his hire
In lingering death, but not by fire!'
But Bill in drunk derision cursed:
'I'll see you on this bonfire first!'
And a wild rain of slugs was dealt
From the revolver at his belt.
As moon and firelight seemed to dim,
They saw the stranger's form dislimn
And fade among the mammoth bones;
And all they found among the stones
Was half a dozen tiny pocks
Where Bill's discharge had chipped the rocks.

IV

Five years passed by. The death of Pete
By drowning had been put to question,
But all our efforts met defeat.
There was no corpse. And the suggestion
That something was extremely wrong
Was proofless, though belief was strong.
Meanwhile the mine at Nistowasis
Was pouring out a golden store
Of bullion for its two grim bosses,
And still they darkly craved for more.

Air transport companies had brought,
To loot that shining reef of quartz,
All of the tools that modern thought
Has fashioned: there were sundry sorts
Of stamp-mills and amalgamators
(Each with its own peculiar failings),
With mercury in stamp-box craters
And cyanide for 'slime' and tailings;
And towering mounds of refuse rose
Where Pete MacLeod had trailed that moose,
While the incessant stamp-mill blows
Rang through the silent miles of spruce.
Since neither road nor railway ran
Into this realm of Smith and Lloyd,
And since the plant—machine and man—
Had come on wings across the void,
Bill Smith, who frequently had flown,
Soon bought a biplane of his own,
And having earned his pilot's papers,
Grew constant in his aery capers.

One August morning, he and Jack
Had put in eighteen holes of golf
At Deer Lodge, before starting back
To see the mine. The pair took off
Just as the Air Field clock struck noon;
At full speed they expected soon
To cross five hundred miles of sky
To where the mine would cheer their eye.

But engine trouble held them stalled
At Norway House for several hours;
And to Jack Lloyd, Bill seemed enthralled
By dark, infuriating Powers:
His tongue lolled like a dog's in drouth,
His blood-shot eyes were wild and staring,
And nervous twitchings at the mouth
Made his fierce glance seem yet more glaring;
While his remarks, as day decreased,
Seemed like the snarls of some wild beast,

The long, slow twilight of the North
Had merged with darkness when at last
The plane was ready to set forth;
And as the light was fully past,
Jack urged it would be wise to stay
At Norway House till break of day.
'You coward!' Bill began to mock.
'The moon comes up at ten o'clock,
Just past the full and plenty bright
To show our way across the night.
You'll get into that plane, you blackguard,
Or learn how lead can cure a laggard!'
More nervous over Bill's wild mood
Than any hazards of the dark,
And feeling that some trouble brewed
From a mad fit so strange and stark,
Jack, in slow silence, got on board;
And just at moonrise, off they soared.

A sea of shadows lay below them,
Silvered with soft, unearthly light;
Only vague outlines served to show them
Their northward way across the night.
Onward they hurtled, flying low;
When suddenly Jack's blood ran cold—
For there before them, all a-glow
With hellish glare as bright as gold,
A sunken, treeless valley shone,
Upon whose floor, outlined with fires,
A grim titanic Skeleton
Leered upward at the gaping fliers.
'That is the place you murdered Pete!'
Said Jack to Bill. 'No, it was you,'
He answered with demented heat;
'Who killed the rascal? Tell me, Who?'
Just at that moment, from the gloom
A huge, white owl, with skull-like eyes,
Swooped like a messenger of doom
And with infuriated cries
Of 'Who? Who? Who?', attacked the pair.
Bill lost control, and through the air
Fell yelling with the twisting plane.
Jack leapt out clear. Bill tried in vain,
With parachute too badly tangled.
The plane took fire. Alive but mangled,
He perished screeching in the fire,
Near where the ashes of Pete's pyre

Still lingered, hideous, moist and gray,
Though five long years had passed away.
We learned all this next day, for Jack
Bailed out too low and broke his back,
But lingered long enough to tell
The truth about their deed of hell,
When fire-rangers, who had sighted
A sudden, flaming plane come down,
Went there at dawn, looked and alighted,
And flew me promptly in from town.

Much of the tale is hard to credit,
But though the yarn is weird and gory,
It was a dying man who said it
And he believed his own dark story;
And when we found charred bones of Pete,
The bloody record seemed complete,
Proving, as said when I began,
That Fate can help us get our man."

The Corporal's Tale *of* THE MEN WHO VANISHED

PROLOGUE

The lean-faced Corporal nodded slow
His confirmation of the tale:
"Yes," he remarked, "I also know
A case where Heaven did not fail
To interpose its Justice, when
A ruthless pair of wicked men
Transgressed the laws of man and God.
But if the Sergeant's case was odd,
This one, I think, was weirder still.
Let me rehearse the tale of ill."
We puffed approval, though unneeded,
And the gaunt Corporal proceeded:

THE CORPORAL'S TALE

I

THE precious pair of whom I spoke
Were 'One-eyed Mike' and 'Scarface Dan',
As reckless, evil-hearted folk
As ever harried mortal man.

Perhaps some thugs are still more black,
Like those chill connoisseurs in crime
Who send your kidnapped children back
One severed finger at a time;
But Mike and Dan were beasts at best.
There were no worse in all the West.
Both were Bulgarians by birth;
As youths they had been jailed for murder,
And might have hanged and slept in earth
Had not a policy absurder
Than all unreason, being fed
By bounties of so much a head
For Western settlers in the raw
Transferred them out to Canada.
By just such tactics of perdition
Canadian agents earned commission,
And left the sequel for our nation
To bear in bitter tribulation.
Mike was a stocky sort of guy,
With glances fiery as a rocket,
Though through a fight his fierce left eye
Was missing wholly from its socket.
Dan, unlike Mike, was lean and bleak,
With grizzled stubble on his chin
And a long scar across his cheek
That gave him an unearthly grin.
After six months of pioneering
Up near The Pas, they tired of clearing

And faded out to Winnipeg,
Where each soon flourished as a yegg.
Then, when police hunts grew too hot,
They sought a less frequented spot,
And hit on a deserted shack
Out in the Rockies, north of Yakh.

II

From this new base of operations,
They started on fresh depredations,
And often vexed with thievish sally
The humble Slovaks of the valley.
Emboldened by the latter's mildness,
They soon went on to greater wildness,
And dared one Sabbath day to search
And rob the entire Slovak church.
The priest was half-way through the Mass
When the two Bulgars, bold as brass,
A six-gun poised in either hand,
Came striding in, with sharp command
To face the walls and raise their arms;
Then, breathing threats of grievous harms,
They quickly took, with ribald mirth,
All each possessed of any worth.
Mike's one fierce eye was full of scorn
And Dan's scarred grin was bleak and pale,
Watching the old priest stand forlorn
Beside the little altar rail.

He lifted up his hand; and lo,
The pair, who were about to go,
Halted in silence as his wrath
Burst in a thundering aftermath.
He cursed their souls to lowest hell;
He cursed their worthless flesh as well;
He cursed their waking hours with pain;
He cursed their sleep with horror's reign;
He cursed their skins with tick and louse;
He cursed the safety of their house—
'On you shall surely come,' he cried,
'A far worse fate than if you died.
With all your human senses keen,
You shall subsist on food obscene
And snarl and howl with beastly breath
In anguished eagerness for death.
Within this day your work of sin
Its penal torment shall begin.
Go! Or, before it is too late,
Kneel down and pray for your sad state!'

III

Giving a laugh, the scornful pair
Strode out and left him standing there,
Mounted their nags and rode away,
And called it a successful day.
Of this affair we Mounties heard
For several weeks no single word;

For Slovak folk, devoutly odd,
Preferred to leave such things to God,
And saw no need to tell police
About such breaches of the peace.
At length the Winnipeg command
Trailed the two miscreants to the land,
And one day I rode out from Yakh
To seize the men and bring them back.
Then, at the village in the valley,
The old priest told me stoically
About the Sunday when his flock
Were rudely robbed and set at mock,
Yet said there was no need to send
For villains who had met their end:
No one had seen them since that time;
God, he was sure, had marked their crime,
And had been pleased on them to vent
Unprecedented punishment.
When I insisted on my ride,
He sent a Slovak as my guide,
Who, with his face a trifle pale,
Soon led me up the mountain trail.

It was a bleak November day
As we rode up that rugged way.
Borne by a piercing autumn wind,
Grey clouds in drifting ribbons thinn'd
Across tall crags of naked stone
That shone as cold as polished bone,

And colder still behind them rose
Fantastic summits white with snows.
I am not a religious sort,
Yet I can candidly report
I sensed upon that mountain path
God's purity and awful wrath.

IV

Around a corner of the trail,
We met the cabin suddenly—
A wooden shack, unkempt and frail,
Beneath a thunder-smitten tree,
A pine whose green had turned instead
To haggard, fateful hues of red.
A battered stable stood behind it
In ruinous dilapidation;
As with the house, we seemed to find it
A thing of utter desolation.
Hemmed round by shining peaks of morning,
They lay beneath a sense of night,
As if the spot, in awful warning,
Were smitten by some nameless blight.
The shack's one door was open wide
Upon a sagging pair of hinges,
And as we slowly stepped inside
I felt my hair-roots stir with twinges
Of some unutterable awe
Scarce called for by the thing I saw.

For little was there to be seen
In that uncanny, dusty room—
Two empty beds, a stove unclean,
Two upturned chairs, a broken broom,
Two suits of clothes, half torn to shreds,
That lay on the dishevelled beds,
And on a table, neatly stacked,
As if to satisfy our search,
The booty we had duly tracked,
The plunder of the Slovak church.
And then I saw, with one glance more,
That all along the cabin floor
Were countless wolf-tracks in the dust,
And marks where, in some fierce disgust,
Wild teeth and claws, their frenzy spreading,
Had gnawed the bed and clawed the bedding.
But of the Bulgars, Mike and Dan,
No single sign was there to scan:
Yes, though we searched on every side,
We could not find them, hair nor hide,
Nor even bloodstains anywhere
To show that wolves had killed them there.
Here were their clothes, and fruits of theft,
But the two men themselves had left,
And, without leaving any trace,
Had simply vanished into space.

Going out back to search the shed,
We found its door was open too,

And there, repulsive to the view,
Two saddle-horses, long since dead,
Were lying on the earthern floor,
While at their mangled haunches tore
Two mangy wolves, two cringing beasts,
Who seemed to loathe such carrion feasts.
Then, as I made a sudden sound,
The wretched creatures turned around
In snarling anger to unsheath
From haggard lips their yellow teeth.
I drew my gun. The Slovak checked me,
And crossed himself in pious awe.
Then, with his finger to direct me,
The thicker, stockier brute I saw
Had glances fiery as a rocket
And one eye missing from its socket,
While his companion wolf was bleak,
Lean as the famine-curst are thin,
With a long scar across his cheek
That gave him an unearthly grin.
They did not fight but only cowered
Back in the corner of a stall;
And there I left them as they glowered,
And did not harm the brutes at all.

V

I'm sure my face was very pale
As we rode back along the trail;

At any rate, I know my mind
Was reeling, and I could not find
An answer to the uncanny sights
Up at that homestead on the heights.
Under the cold November skies,
Beneath those awful mountain summits,
I thought of man as one who dies,
A feeble beast, whose reason plummets
Only the surface of a sea
Of spiritual mystery.
What I had seen I scarce could tell,
Yet somehow knew a moving swell
From holy seas beyond my ken
Had washed the sin-stained shores of men,
And sweeping up along the beach
Had touched a spot beyond the reach
Of common tides and common reason
To punish evil in its season.
Yet when I turned in my report
I gave no version of that sort.
My humble Slovak guide and I
Could never hope to satisfy
A Philistine intelligence
With tales that somehow had no sense.
So to my chief I merely said:
'The men are missing. Likely dead.
We found the homestead wolf-infested.
No doubt the pair are now digested.'

That's what I told him. But I know
That after all it wasn't so,
And that it was my privilege
To stand upon the outer edge
Of a stupendous mystery
Beyond the guess of you and me."

The Butcher's Tale
of
THE FORT HENRY TUNNEL

PROLOGUE

The butcher shivered, and a trace
Of melancholy nightmare spread
Across his plump Teutonic face,
While in disquietude he said:
"There are conditions that appal
In tales so supernatural,
Yet I am certain, without error,
That there is more of mortal terror
In purely physical affright.
I can't forget one dreadful night
When, without ghosts or ghouls hell-painted,
I faced such horror that I fainted.
Since themes of terror are your dish,
I'll tell the story, if you wish."
As no one ventured to comment,
He took our silence for consent;
And with a shudder of his own
He told his tale in halting tone:

I

THE worst experience of my life
Was at Fort Henry, long ago
During the War, when bitter strife
Estranged our countries. Then, although
The sentence was but slightly earned,
I found myself at last interned.
The trouble was that Hermann Klein,
An old compatriot of mine
Back home in Baden, came to me
One autumn night in Napanee,
Where I was working in a mill,
And lodged with me. It was a thrill
To meet good Hermann once again.
I was the happiest of men,
Until he urged me, turned advisor,
To cross the sea and serve the Kaiser.
He then was on his way, he said,
But I refused, and claimed instead
That I had found in Canada
Congenial work and life and law.
He was arrested two days later,
Trying to reach the States from Bath,
And I, alleged collaborator,
Likewise incurred official wrath,

Although my sole offence, he swore,
Was housing him two nights before.
  Crumbling Fort Henry, cold and damp,
Became our concentration camp,
Along with several hundred others,
Who hailed us as Germanic brothers.
It was a fortress, old and chill,
Sunk in the summit of a hill
That westward looked on Kingston town
And to the east sloped slowly down
To a deep inlet, bleak and grey,
That bore the name of Dead Man's Bay.
Southward, the broad St. Lawrence reeled;
North, lay the plains of Barriefield.
The fort, I learned, had been erected
A century since, but, long neglected,
Had mouldered with the frost's abuse
Until war claimed its sudden use,
Disturbing, in their dank abode,
Spider and beetle, slug and toad.
When Klein and I were landed there,
There'd been scant effort at repair,
For moss was thick upon the roof
And ancient doors were foul with rust
And tottering battlements gave proof
That mortar had dissolved to dust,
While deep along the great dry moat
That hemmed the 'Lower Fort' around

Whole strips of wall had lost a coat
Of ashlars, tumbled on the ground.
But high above, the sentries walked,
Patrolling all the wind-swept hill;
And we, within the ruin, talked,
Or dreamed that we were free men still.

II

The oldest legend of the place
Was that a secret tunnel lay
Under the fortress' deepest base
And down the hill to Dead Man's Bay.
Just where it was, no person knew.
Even the guards had no idea.
In daydreams, when our minds were blue,
That tunnel was a panacea;
For thus in many a magic vision
We fled reality's derision
And slipped by ceiling, wall, or floor
Into that wondrous corridor,
Under the moat and down the slope,
An avenue to life and hope.

The ground floor casemate farthest east,
A darkened cell, as black as ink
And hardly fit to house a beast,
Was known to guardsmen as the 'Clink',
A prison cell where men unruly
In close confinement suffered duly.

Here Hermann Klein and I were placed
One late November day in haste
For having dared, with restless skill,
To make a sturdy home-made still
And boil a mash, high-proof and keen,
With makings from the fort canteen,
In hope to pass the waning year
With some resource of liquid cheer.
But soon the nosey adjutant
Had rooted out our little plant,
And so, instead of Schnapps to drink,
We had a sudden dose of 'Clink'.

Once in the dungeon, Hermann Klein
Professed to me he liked it fine
To have a chance to check the place
And in the floor to find a trace
Of that old tunnel. Other men
Had told him, ever and again,
That near the north wall, under test,
One spot rang hollower than the rest:
A shaft was underneath the floor
If only they could find the door.
He had come ready, you perceive,
For he was clever and designing—
With tallow-candles in his sleeve
And matches in his trouser-lining—
And with the aid of such a light
We searched the casemate half the night.

It seemed in vain. The floor rang hollow
In one spot, but it did not follow
That it would open at our will.
For hours, the whole result was nil.
Klein was undaunted, and at last
A still more searching gaze was cast
On three brass spikes spaced fairly wide
Breast-high upon the northern side.
We'd thought them clothes-pegs, but now Klein
Supposed them part of some design
To lock the stone beneath our feet,
And so he tried, in ways discreet,
To pull them slowly farther out
(A trick which failed), and then with care
To push them in. With sudden shout
He grabbed me, for a winding stair
Was at our feet, where one huge block
Swung on a pivot in the floor
And showed a shaft of limestone rock
Gape downward fifty feet or more.
'At last!' cried Klein. 'The tale was true!
Friend Wagner, we're as good as through.'
And so, with hearts as light as air,
We started down the winding stair,
Fresh from the tools of long ago.
But as we hurried on below,
A sudden thud above my head
Told that the stone had closed once more

And numbered us among the dead
Unless the path lay clear before.
'Mein Gott!' said Hermann. 'That is bad.
But we shall soon be out, my lad.'
  The staircase-shaft sank vertical,
For fifty feet, as I have said,
There then began a narrow hall
To east-northeast that overhead
Was dank with seepage from the hill,
Blotching the ceiling, low and chill.
The floor sloped steeply, it was clear;
It was the passage of our dreams;
Perhaps our liberty was near!
And so by two small candles' beams
(For each of us now bore a light)
We hurried on in happy flight.

III

I shudder in remembrance yet
At the dark horror that we met
As we drew near to Dead Man's Bay
By that dark, subterranean way.
For first a rank, reptilian smell
Rose like a sudden blast from hell,
And then, almost at once with this,
A sleepy, thousand-throated hiss
Filled all the place from side to side
And set us gaping, horrified.

Just at our feet, as we descended,
The honest limestone pavement ended,
And the whole passage, two feet deep,
Was filled with vipers half asleep,
A monstrous, writhing, reptile mass
That here had crept in swarms to pass
The winter, kenneled in the dark;
While far beyond them, like a spark,
A low, dim exit we could see,
Cluttered with mouldering débris,
For half the roof had fallen in
Where once a way for men had been,
And only left a gap in view
Where rats or snakes could wriggle through.
Such was our plight. Far back, behind,
Cold limestone barred us from our kind,
Sentenced to starve, without a doubt,
Unless we found some passage out;
And now before us writhed and hissed
Such horror as no moralist
In dreams of grimmest resolution
E'er planned for sinners' retribution.
Then as I paused and, gaping, gripped
My candle tighter, Hermann slipped
And with a scream would wake the dead
Dove open-mouthed, with arms outspread,
Like some raw diver at the lakes,
Full in the heaving mass of snakes.

Aroused to fury by his fall,
They bit him fiercely everywhere
And over him began to crawl—
I could not even see his hair.
Then a last, dying flurry smote
My friend. I saw him rise and stand
With twenty serpents round his throat
And snake-teeth fleshed in either hand.
But though a single viper's bite
May seldom serve to kill a man,
The venom of such hosts had might
To poison a leviathan;
And Hermann sank to rise no more,
While hordes of hideous weavers wove
Their woof above him on the floor
Until his strength no longer strove.

One of my life's near-worst mistakes
Was waiting, gazing there, in terror,
For an approaching wave of snakes
Almost destroyed me in my error.
I saw them coming, just in time,
And turning round, began to climb
With frenzied haste from that abyss,
And still behind me heard them hiss.
My flickering candle sputtered out
As I raced madly up the steep,
Yet still I groped my way about
Like some wild madman in his sleep,

And blundered on in my despair
Until I reached the spiral stair.
Then up the dusty steps I sped
Until at last, with hope nigh dead,
I crouched beneath that massive stone
That held me prisoner. With a groan,
I sat, and marked my spirits melt
And all my fancies seethe and rankle:
I heard no sound, and yet I felt
A viper coiling round my ankle—
But when I went to kick it free,
My foot encountered vacancy.
In spite of all, I had the sense
Of snaky presences. Suspense
Clutched at my bursting heart and brain
Until I fainted with the pain.

IV

How long I swooned, I cannot say;
But all at once the stone gave way
Above me there; the fresh air blew
Upon me, and a face peered through.
'One of them's here,' a sharp voice said.
'It's Wagner, and he looks half dead.'
I knew the voice too well, I grant—
It was that nosey adjutant—
And yet to me he looked so good
I could have hugged him where he stood.

Finding the prisoners in the Clink
Had vanished, he begins to think
Of some old tunnel, closely checks it,
And so, like us, he finds the exit.
Half-crazed, I stammered out my tale,
And ten men down the backward trail
Went armed with hip-boots, clubs, and rakes
And got Klein's body from the snakes.

Next day at ten I was paraded
Before the Commandant, to whom
I told (my face with horror faded)
The story of my comrade's doom.
He listened grimly till I ceased,
Then asked me, in a tone of warning:
'Why seek escape? You've been released.
The order came through just this morning.
And though your gaol-break needs rebuff,
I think we'll pass the whole thing over.
You must have suffered quite enough—
You didn't spend your time in clover.'

And so I left the Fort behind;
But till I die, within my mind
A secret shaft is hidden deep,
And often, waking or asleep,
A stone will move, dark steps descend,
And through black tunnels without end
I walk and hear once more, aghast,
The hissing horror of the past."

THE LAWYER'S TALE

of

THE ABANDONED FARMHOUSE

PROLOGUE

The quietest of all the party
That sat and talked around the fire
Was a pale lawyer, far from hearty,—
A man who looked as if some dire
And sinister experience
Had harried him with pain intense.
"Believe in ghosts?" the drover laughed:
"Not I, my lads."
The lawyer frowned:
"If you are right, then I am daft;
Because I've seen one, I'll be bound!"
A sudden eerie silence fell,
There in that Manitou hotel.
Some disbelieved, but all could see
He had a story. Therefore, we,
Avid for tales of mirth or woe,
Urged him to tell of it, and so
The local lawyer, grim and pale,
Told quietly his ghostly tale:

THE LAWYER'S TALE

I

"IT was the worst year of the drought,"
The lawyer said, and looked more grim,
"That Jacob Beynon-Jones came out
To find his lost twin-brother Jim.
I still can see his hawk-like face,
Its unforgettable design
With brow of most excessive space
And nose grotesquely aquiline.
It was a scorching August day
When he arrived in Manitou
By taxi, and was forced to stay
When the rear axle cracked clean through.
He was a most impatient cuss
And kicked up an ungodly fuss,
Demanding, furious and profane,
To go at once to Deloraine.
As I was going out that way
On business, in my Ford coupé,
I asked the man to come with me
The hundred miles, for company.
Feeling the obligation strong,
He told me, as we drove along,
The reasons for his present trip;
For he had just arrived by ship

From England, and had come out West
Upon a most surprising quest.
'My name is Beynon-Jones,' he said.
'I have a lost twin-brother, Jim.
So like myself, from heel to head,
That none can tell me quite from him.
Back home in Devonshire as youths,
Black rivalry in love estranged us.
Through ten grey years of lies and truths,
In that, at least, Time has not changed us.
I wed my blue-eyed Susan, Sir,
But Jim one night, as I had feared,
Impersonated me with her
As husband, and then disappeared,
Taking my honour and my cash
To distant lands in one fell smash.
The shock of fortune so unkind
Unsettled my poor Susan's mind
And broke my heart. For many a day
I brooded on the runaway.
No trace of Jim was found abroad,
And ten long years of sorrow gnawed
My heart in silence. Susan died
Only last May, and it is queer
That day a cable from this side—
I SHALL BE WAITING FOR YOU HERE—
Reached me from Jim. The place, I saw,
Was Deloraine, in Canada.

Business took time to clear away—
Ties are not broken in a day.
And now I trust I'm not too late
To meet the brother that I hate!'
Then suddenly, as breezes flapped
His coat aside, with some alarm
I saw a black revolver strapped
Securely underneath his arm.

We had a hundred miles to go;
And as we neared the range of drought,
All vegetation ceased to grow,
The starveling harvests petered out.
Till fields by Deloraine were just
A lifeless waste of hot, grey dust.

We sought the station to enquire
About the sender of the wire.
The agent of the C. P. R.
Smiled as I brought my caller in;
Then almost dropped his black cigar
Half-smoked, and checked his friendly grin,
Staring at my companion's face
Like one who could not quite define
That brow of most excessive space,
That nose grotesquely aquiline.
'My God,' he said, in sober tones,
'I thought it was Jim Beynon-Jones.'
'I am his brother,' was the answer.
'Tell me, as quickly as you can, Sir,

Where I can find him.'

'I suppose

He's on his farm near Vulture Nose,
Southwest of us nigh forty miles.
Three months ago he called in here,
Excited-like and full of smiles,
To send a cable; but I fear
He hasn't been in town since then.
He's one of the unluckiest men
You ever saw. This cursèd drought
Has dried the plains completely out.
Most of the farmers out his way
Have left their farms this many a day;
Then both of his young children died
Of "flu" last autumn, more's the pity;
His wife then took a one-way ride
Back to her folks at Crystal City;
But Jim refused to leave the spot;
He lives alone there on the farm,
Feeding himself on God knows what.
I hope he doesn't come to harm.'

Sardonic satisfaction came
Into the brother's hawk-like eyes:
'Come, Mr. Jukes, and join my game!
Let's give old Jim a real surprise!
It's just an hour or so past noon.
Your car will get us out there soon.'

There was a menace in his tone
That thrilled me with a nameless fear.
I did not like him. That was clear.
And yet I could not hold my own
Against his dark, hypnotic eye
That mastered me, I knew not why.
And so, with feelings vaguely chill.
I started off against my will.

II

As we pushed on from Deloraine
Into the endless, treeless plain,
A slow, hot wind began to rise
And stain the sunlight in the skies
With weird apocalyptic gloom
From stifling clouds of livid grit,
As if the smoke of final Doom
Were breathing from the nether Pit.
Like ashes on the floor of Hell,
Grey dust kept sifting ceaselessly
Across the half-hid parallel
Of buried fence and ditch, as we,
Turning our gaze from side to side,
Gaped at the blasted countryside.
In bald expanses, left and right,
The marl from which the soil had blown
Shone sterile in that lurid light,
The colour of decaying bone.

No honest desert was this land—
Where prickly pear and cactus grew
In smiling sunlight in the sand—
But the grey corpse of plains I knew,
Plains where strong men had won with toil
Abundant food from fertile soil;
But now a dead community
Lay stifled there in dust and heat,
Shrouded, with grim diablerie,
Under a dusty winding-sheet.

Warm dust was in my eyes and hair;
It clogged my nostrils and my mouth;
And ever hotter grew the air
Out of some furnace in the South.
By dun, deserted homes we passed,
Into the suffocating blast,
And saw the leeward roofs all draped
With drifts of dust; and underneath,
The homes' dark doors and windows gaped
Like cavities in dead men's teeth.

'The road-gauge there reads thirty-five
Since we pulled out of Deloraine.'
Said Beynon-Jones. 'If Jim's alive
And at his place, I think it's plain
We're near him now. I wish the Devil
Would help us find him, on the level!'
As if it heard the thing he said,
Our engine coughed, and passed out dead.

III

For hours I tried to start once more—
Checked up on spark-plugs, gas, and water.
She wouldn't budge. And Jacob swore
That Hell itself had surely bought her.
Leaving her there beside the road,
We set out for the nearest farm.
Over the drifted fence we strode,
Straight to the house; and in alarm
I saw the sun's infernal light
Was darkening to actual night.
The farm-yard was a gruesome place
Under that failing light of day.
I wished myself, without disgrace,
A good five thousand miles away.
Nigh buried in the dusty waves
Were ploughs and harrows, rakes and waggons,
Projecting from their sandy graves
Like skeletons of primal dragons.
But the gaunt house was still more eerie,
Bleak and unutterably dreary.
The drifting sand-blast from that home
Had worn away all paint, and left
A desolate grey monochrome
Of leprous planking, warped and cleft
By baleful heat; and at the door
The dust lay three feet deep or more.

We walked around to see the back
Of that grim house, but marked no sign
Of any life. The rooms were black.
'Well,' said my comrade, 'I decline
To walk to Deloraine to-night.
You get that hamper and a light.
Beds on deserted farms are cheap.
At least we'll have a place to sleep;
And when the morning comes, no doubt
We'll promptly find our way about.'
The back door yielded at a touch,
And with electric torch in hand
We carried in our lunch: not much
For hunger's clamorous demand,
But welcome fare. Without delay
We spread it on a dusty table,
And stowed our bread and cheese away
With such poor cheer as we were able.
It was a melancholy room
In which we sat on creaking chairs
And turned our flashlight on the gloom
From dusty stove to dusty stairs;
And though most obvious to see
Were signs of utter poverty,
I seemed to sense, I must aver,
Some presence far more sinister,
And shuddering smelt, with pale dismay,
A nameless fetor of decay.

Just off the kitchen where we sat,
A bedroom, with a double bed,
Stood waiting. 'I am ripe for that,'
Said Beynon-Jones. 'Me too,' I said.
So, without stopping to undress,
We lay down in our weariness
As simply as a pair of sheep,
And fell into a troubled sleep.

IV

When I awoke, it still was night.
Through eastward window panes the moon
Was pouring an unearthly light.
But not for this had I so soon
Wakened from sleep. Unearthly talk
Came from a figure by the door,
A towering Form that seemed to walk
With shambling feet across the floor,
And point impatient to the stairs
And gibber loudly and rejoice.
My startled bed-mate said his prayers:
'By Heaven,' he said, 'I know that voice!'
Then, as if caught by some dark force,
He rose up quickly from the bed.
'I've come!' he cried, in accents hoarse;
And followed where that Something led.

Armed with the flashlight, I came too,
Drawn by the strangeness of it all.
Up the dark stairs they passed from view
Into a bare, unfurnished hall.
There came a burst of crazy laughter
From Beynon-Jones; and then I saw,
Before us, dangling from a rafter,
With sagging neck and grinning jaw,
A corpse, half-rotten, to supplant
Our recent ghastly visitant.
And even in that greenish face
My gaping horror could divine
A brow of most excessive space,
A nose grotesquely aquiline—
A diabolic parody
On him who had come there with me.
This was the end of our strange ride:
To be alone at midnight there
In that dread house with such a pair—
A madman and a suicide.
Redoubled laughter chilled my ear;
Then Beynon-Jones became more grim
And beckoned with a maniac leer:
'Come, Mr. Jukes, meet Brother Jim!'
My trembling fingers dropped the light,
That jarred to darkness as it fell.
My hair rose up. I turned to flight;
Groped to the stairs; and with a yell,

Went stumbling down the steps like mad,
Out of the house and towards the car;
And then, behind me, heard the pad
Of running feet. It was not far
To where the car stood; but my knees,
Turning to water, left me lame.
My very heart-blood seemed to freeze
As through the moonlight towards me came
My crazy comrade, weirdly black,
With the cadaver on his back,
And on his face such hate and scorn,
Such hideous likeness to the other
In livid hue, I could have sworn
The corpse was carrying its brother.
'Lend me a hand,' the figure said.
'The rumble-seat's the place for Jim.'
So there we propped his nodding head
And made the cushions soft for him.
Into the front seat then we climbed;
Somehow or other, in my heart,
I knew Hell had that engine primed
And that the car would surely start.
  At my first touch she gave a bound.
Quickly I turned her nose around,
And started back across the plain,
Racing, hell-bent, for Deloraine.
My nerves in no time were a wreck;
For how could sanity keep sweet

With mania's breath upon my neck
And carrion in the rumble-seat?
On, ever faster, past control,
We neared the town across the prairie,
And crashed into a Hydro pole
Beside the civic cemetery.

When consciousness returned again—
A whole week later, so they said—
I found myself laid up in bed
With every muscle full of pain
And forty stitches in my forehead
And both my arms done up in splints,
And a vague sense of something horrid
That I'd been through, until from hints
The doctor made, the whole weird, black
Night of appalling fear came back,
And then I learned that when we spilled
Against that pole, my man was killed,
And one grey grave had served to bury
Both brothers in one cemetery.
How I escaped is far from plain.
I'm glad that I'm alive and sane."

THE FIRST FARMER'S TALE

of

THE DRIFTING CORPSE

PROLOGUE

Right in the centre by the fire,
A farmer sat, a stalwart Swede,
Who looked as if no toil could tire
A man of such a virile breed.
Unmoved, he heard the lawyer tell
His story of the haunted farm.
"Still worse than that," he said, "befell
A woman, with the grim alarm
Of Hell, right at my neighbour's place.
Through all the course of all my days,
I never knew of anyone
Who faced such things as she has done
And still retained a stable mind
For intercourse with humankind."
  "I still am dubious," said the drover,
"About these yarns of eerie terror.
Perhaps your tale will win me over
And quite convince me of my error."
  "One's faith," he answered, "must go far.
I shall persuade you if I can."
And with a puff at his cigar,
The massive, blue-eyed Swede began:

I

THE setting for the affair malign
Was on the farm just next to mine,
Where fields and whispering poplars join
Along the broad Assiniboine
Just where its course runs full and freely
A few miles north and east of Elie.
Here Ivan Bykoff lived alone
In a low cottage of his own
Where poplar-leaves forever shiver
Along the margin of the river.
Ivan was Russian, stout and squat,
His lips were full, his eyes were hot,
His straight black hair was thick and sleek,
His mouth professed a smirk oblique,—
A bold, insinuating smile
As if his heart were full of guile;
And certainly all through a life
Much marred with interludes of drabbing
He was too handy with a knife
And was a dirty man for stabbing.

He had a younger brother Paul,
Who lived six hundred miles up-stream
Just where a little waterfall
Broke the dull river's muddy dream

Near Binscarth—for though crows might fly
Between them through the clear blue sky
In upwards of two hundred miles,
The river's curving course beguiles
Three times that distance as it swings
Through countless slow meanderings.
Paul had a buxom Polish wife,
A warm, deep-bosomed, blue-eyed blonde,
But though he loved her as his life
And she of him seemed just as fond,
No fruit of little children came
To bless his union with his dame;
And so at times there was a trace
Of hunger on her handsome face
And fits of moody discontent
That vaguely came and slowly went.
Into their Eden, Ivan broke
One day in spring, and though he spoke
Of harrows, ploughs, and new seed grain,
Somehow to Marja it was plain
His hot, moist gaze was always prest
Upon her brow and throat and breast.
In brief, by ways obscurely human,
Within a week he won the woman,
And when she had agreed to flight,
He took his knife one stormy night
And stabbing Paul with eyes a-gleam
Sank his dead body in the stream.

Then by the C. N. R. genteelly
He took fair Marja down to Elie,
And in his shack, as man and wife,
They lived without a hint of strife.
When Binscarth learned that Paul was gone,
The people put the Mounties on
The pair that went by C. N. R.,
But no enquiry could get far.
There was no body—hence no murder.
'And what,' said Ivan, 'is absurder
Than worry over live men's fates?
Paul's on a visit to the States.
And is it a police concern
If his good wife, till his return,
Should come and visit with his brother,
The offspring of a common mother?'
No matter how police might frown,
They couldn't break that story down.

II

Two months of guilty love went by,
More mad through mutual sense of sin;
But one warm evening in July
As Ivan, with a happy grin
Sat beside Marja on the bank
And watched the radiant sun that sank,
While his plump paramour beside him
With pensive gaze of passion eyed him,

A drifting Something slowly rounded
The upper bend of poplars sweet
And in unerring onset grounded
In the low shallows at their feet.
A quick grimace of horror warps
The woman's face: it is a corpse,
A naked body, white and bloated,
That in the muddy stream had floated,
Furnishing food to fish and leeches
Along the river's slimy beaches.
They rose and gave a closer look.
Then Marja screamed, turned pale, and shook,
Till Ivan caught her, lest she fall.
'Ivan,' she shrieked, 'it's Paul, it's Paul!'
For even in the rotting face
A recognizing glance could trace,
Plain for all humankind to scan,
The likeness of the murdered man.
Ivan looked black. 'By Heaven,' he said,
'He comes to plague us though he's dead.
And if that face were recognized,
Our guilt would soon be advertised.'
Then furious, but with nerves of steel,
He raised his heavy, hob-nailed heel
And stamped upon his brother's face,
Seeking thus harshly to erase
All human semblance that might be
A clue to his identity.

Then, to dislodge him from the shoal,
He took a sturdy ten-foot pole,
Pushed off the body from the shore,
And gave it to the stream once more.

III

Meanwhile, across the western sky,
Fierce clouds of thunder mounted high,
Blotting the sunset's rosy light—
And with the tempest came the night.
Snug in the cabin lay the pair
With windows locked and door close-barred,
And watched the lightning's dazzling glare,
And heard the thunder rolling hard,
While on the roof the wind and rain
Beat out a clamorous refrain.
Protected in strong Ivan's arms,
Marja had lost the day's alarms;
When suddenly, with sense of shock,
They heard a loud though muffled knock
That even above the tempest's roar
Kept pounding on the bolted door,
And groping fingers seemed to snatch
And rattle at the metal latch.
A sudden, speechless horror gripped
The pair, and kept them frozen-lipped.
And now the rapping came again—
This time upon the window-pane.

Leaving the bed, they came to see
Who the strange visitor might be
That on a night of wind and storm
Came rapping thus. They saw a form
That in the murky shades of night
Reached, as by touch and not by sight,
Inhuman hands that thumped abuse
And tried to pry the window loose.
There came a livid lightning flash,
And by its glare, beyond the sash,
Their staring eyes could clearly trace
A mangled, rotted, sightless face
And pale, disintegrating hands
Stretched in importunate demands.
'It's Paul, by Heaven!' Ivan said.
'Why can't he die when he is dead?'
Then wildly from the wall he drew
A small repeating .22,
And sent a stream of leaden rain
Exploding through the window-pane;
Yet saw that horrid figure stay
Though half one hand was shot away,
Nor did it falter or depart
With forty bullets in its heart.
Minute by minute, hour by hour,
Impelled by some unholy power,
It beat upon the bolted door
And tried the window-sash once more

And even thrust an arm in vain
In through the shattered window-pane.
By midnight, Ivan's nerve was broken;
And though no further word was spoken,
He tore his hair with laugh inhuman,
Took up a knife and stabbed the woman,
And with his face one twisted leer
Slit his own throat from ear to ear.

IV

Such was the story Marja brought me
Early next morning, when she sought me
Across the sodden fields of mud,
Faint with fatigue and loss of blood.
Sobs of repentance racked her too;
Her prayers to heaven were warm and true,
Invoking holy aid to save
Her spirit from a sinner's grave.
All through the night, in much distress,
She had maintained her consciousness,
And would have sought me, sure as sin,
But her frail courage, past a doubt,
Could face the bloody dead within
But not the pale, white dead without,
Who still assailed the little shack
From side to side, from front to back,
But, when at last the first sun shone,
Turned to the river and was gone.

That same day, helped by the police,
I tried to give that body peace,
And found it grounded on some sand
Out in the river, close at hand.
  It was a case that seemed to stir
The Mounties and the coroner;
But I maintained, (and proved a winner)
Marja was victim more than sinner.
Both Paul and Ivan sleep in earth
And walk no more; but far from mirth,
Whene'er I see the aspens shiver
Down in the copse along the river,
I think of that unearthly night
That changed a woman's hair to white,
And waking, too, an inner sense
Of all-consuming penitence,
Made her, until her days are done,
A shrinking, wan-faced, black-robed nun,
Who in a convent lives in prayer
And penance, out at St. Norbert."

The School-inspector's Tale
of
THE COURTING OF OLGA KARG

PROLOGUE

Our host had thrown a log or two
Of birch upon the blazing fire;
In silence for a space, we drew
Upon our pipes, and seemed to tire
Of telling stories by the hour.
But interest returned with power
When Casey, as our talk's director,
Turned to the wrinkled school-inspector:
"You know this country pretty well,"
Said he, "and possibly can tell
Whether our fifty races blend
Into one nation. Do they end
In this new land their ancient woe
And bitter feuds from long ago?"
The school-inspector smiled: "I guess
The answer's neither No nor Yes.
But there are changes. As a rule,
They issue from the local school.
But sometimes . . . Well, a tale of sorts
Is worth a bushel of reports."

He paused, with glances promissory.
To check him had been rude or mulish.
And so began his little story
How Olga Karg taught out at Kulish.

THE SCHOOL-INSPECTOR'S TALE

I

EAST of the long Duck Mountain range,
Just where its high morainic ridges
Drop steeply down, and mad brooks change
To long, slow rivers, thronged with midges,
A Slavic hamlet, Kulish, lies
Among the stunted birch and spruce,
And with its hay-fields occupies
The haunts of beaver, bear, and moose.
A narrow road of miry dirt
Leads eastward, out to Ethelbert;
But otherwise, broad forests bound
The small community around.
Humble Ukrainians and Poles—
In all, about a hundred souls—
Have there hewn out a small domain
And built their homes, white-washed and plain,
With low-thatched roofs and stacks of hay
Piled in the ancient Slavic way.

Out near the borders of the clearing,
A small Canadian school-house stands
To din into small children's hearing
The language of our Western Lands
And some slight modicum of learning
To make them citizens, discerning
A wider world of human good
Beyond that hamlet in the wood.

Here, one September, came as teacher
Young Olga Karg, aged twenty-two—
As plumply ravishing a creature
As Wesley College e'er put through—
With voice as luscious as a melon
And the ripe curves of Spartan Helen.
Her eyes were blue as summer pools,
Her curly hair was chestnut brown;
And sudden interest in schools
Smote the chief bachelor in town—
A tall young Pole named Zygmunt Janik,
Whose charms and eager interest
Might well induce delightful panic
In any normal woman's breast.

But to the hamlet's blank surprise
She looked on him with scornful eyes,
And would with bitterness disparage
His merest hint of love or marriage.
'You are a Pole,' she'd say with scorn,
'And I, a pure Ukrainian, born

In straight descent from that great Hetman
Who once beat Poland. Don't forget, man,
The old injustice of your race!
To me it would be black disgrace
To sell my true Ukrainian soul
In marriage to a tyrant Pole.'
But Zygmunt in remonstrance said:
'Surely the old feuds of our clans
Are now, in this new country, dead,
And we are both Canadians—
Born here on Manitoban soil
And freed from all that Old World broil!
Perhaps you think you have been foolish
To come and teach out here in Kulish,
And do not want to settle down
In such a tiny backwoods town;
Or, since you have such stores of knowledge
And in the city went to college
For four proud years, you feel above me,
And so won't condescend to love me.
This is the truth, and not some hate
Traced back to 1648!'
Olga was furious in denials
Of such provoking accusations,
And poured upon his head the vials
Of her soft-voiced recriminations;
But flamed so radiant that he swore
He wished to be her mate the more.

All winter long he wooed in vain;
His honest courting only seemed
To stir up more intense disdain;
Yet there were moments when he deemed
A softer light was in her glance
While she dealt out some verbal whipping,
As if she stormed, because, perchance,
She felt her resolution slipping.
Thus he still kept his courage up
Till spring brought back the buttercup.

II

It was a sunny day in June
That settled Olga's fate at last.
From the school-windows came the croon
Of learning's one enthusiast
In Kulish, as she gently sought
To get the daily lesson taught.
Across the road was Zygmunt's place.
That afternoon, he patched the roof
Of his old barn, yet kept his face
Turned towards the school, where, so aloof
From all his passionate regard,
A girl taught—soft, and yet so hard.

Just down below the school-house hill,
Wild strawberries grew ripe and thick,
Tempting the little folks to fill
Their hungry mouths. Arithmetic

And history could not compete
With provender so fresh and sweet.
And many a little pupil's brain
Strayed sadly from the appointed book,
While Olga struggled on in vain
To win attention, for his look
Told that the mind beneath his thatch
Was absent in the berry-patch.
  When four o'clock released them all,
A tousled score of girls and boys
In sudden, loud recessional
Went whooping forth. Their merry noise
Receded in a breakneck rush
To where the fruit grew low and lush.
There followed silence for a space . .
While berries at a headlong pace
Were slipping down each little throat
From Nature's one-course *table d'hôte;*
For hungry children, beyond doubt,
Would even rather eat than shout.
  But all at once a piercing scream
Brought Olga rushing to the door.
She looked: it seemed some evil dream
Had cursed a day so fair before.
Among the frightened children ran
A baby bear; and, just beyond,
A tall, black she-bear rose to scan
The little black-furred vagabond;

Then, sensing peril for her cub,
She shambled out in angry error,
As fierce as black Beelzebub
To all those children in their terror.
Appalled at their impending doom,
The teacher seized the school-house broom;
And with her own risks quite forgot,
She ran undaunted to the spot.

III

Zygmunt had likewise heard their shriek
Of panic from the berry-patch,
And saw their peril, from the peak
Of his log barn, then rushed to snatch
A hasty axe up, on his way
To hold the wrathful bear at bay.
'Run to the school-house, all of you,'
He shouted as he reached the scene.
Swiftly, on feet of fear, they flew,—
All except Olga, who, with mien
Transformed by horror, love and pride,
Remained to battle by his side.

Then, in dull rage at all things human,
The she-bear first attacked the woman,
Who slammed her broomstick on the snout
Of the black monster, while the man
Swinging his axe up, with a shout,
Slashed at its head, but struck a span

Beneath its ear and gashed its shoulder.
Then, as blood spurted, growing bolder,
He drew near for a second stroke
But frenzy in the bear awoke:
Roaring with pain, it reared and struck
The wheeling axe and sent it flying.
Zygmunt then turned, with desperate pluck,
And took up Olga's broom, relying
On its frail strength in time of danger;
But the grim bear, with one fierce bound,
Hurled its black bulk upon the stranger
And threw him headlong to the ground.
With bear above and man beneath,
His left arm felt those mighty teeth;
But Olga meanwhile had retrieved
His missing weapon and perceived
His peril. With her arms a-strain,
She sank the axe in Bruin's brain,
And panting, watched the enemy
Topple and die convulsively.
Half across Zygmunt's body lay
The mighty carcass; and in haste
She tugged it feverishly away.
Zygmunt was groaning, pale as paste;
And bloody currents, bright and warm,
Were gushing from his mangled arm.
In anguish at that savage hurt,
Whose blood-flow bore a mortal threat,

She tore quick strips from off her skirt,
And fashioning a tourniquet
Held back the fatal tide, then dressed
The arm with grief but ill suppressed.
Still pale, but with a wistful smile,
Zygmunt lay looking at her, while,
With strong but trembling hands, she finished
Her task with sorrow undiminished.
'Olga!' he murmured. At her name,
And at the hunger in his eyes,
Alternate white and scarlet came
Across her cheeks. She went to rise;
But, kneeling yet, with gaze grown tender,
She gave a sobbing little moan,
And pressed in sudden, soft surrender
Her quivering lips upon his own.
Then, in recoil from all alarms,
She fainted outright in his arms.

IV

Love hath His will in ways tyrannic.
Olga became, eight years ago,
A very happy Mrs. Janik,
And since then, every year or so,
Love's never-failing fires have sent
Her home some infant increment—
Some girl or boy, to grow and play
On Christmas Eve among the hay

Beneath a Slavic Christmas-tree,
And having gorged on *pierohí*,
Kutya, and fish, at length to pass
Out to a solemn midnight Mass.
But still, in fashions hard to scan,
They also grow Canadian:
Seven-year Olga, sweet and cool,
Takes six-year Zygmunt by the hand
And goes across the road to school,
Where a new teacher, plain and bland,
Builds up a slow Canadian nation
On patient sills of education.
Old hates die hard? Perhaps they do.
But love may help us muddle through!"

The Bus Driver's Tale

of

THE MAGYAR VIOLINIST

PROLOGUE

The long-faced driver of the bus
Grew restive at this tale of love,
And in impatience turned to us
And crossly said: "By Heaven above,
Some people have the notion still
That every Jack must have his Jill
In this imperfect world below;
But I have found it isn't so,
And many a case of adoration
Ends in sheer heart-break and frustration.
I call to mind a tragic case
In which a lad of parts and grace
Was destined to a tragic end.
I knew him somewhat, as a friend,
And so can vouch for every fact,
And saw, myself, the final act."
The merchant roused a bit at this.
"Speak on!" he said with emphasis,
"For while there is no use pretending
We don't prefer a happy ending,

Yet we aren't children. We can face
The fact of suffering, in its place."
And so that melancholy man,
The driver of the bus, began:

THE BUS DRIVER'S TALE

I

WHEN I was young, I used my muscle
Out with a big construction gang
Building a railway north of Russell,
And came to know the bitter pang
Of winter frost, likewise the pain
Of summer suns that bake the brain.
We were a sturdy group of roughs,
Busy (on hash and pork-and-beans)
In gouging gravel from the bluffs
And filling in the deep ravines.
We slept in bunk-cars on a siding,
Sun-blistered box-cars, rudely fashioned,
And there the Chinese cook, dividing
Such provender as had been rationed,
Kept all content on copious fare
Who through the months were working there.
Yet sometimes, when, just in the offing,
I heard the big steam shovel coughing,

It seemed a lonely life to me,
Though on the prairie I could see
A village throng of furry loafers—
Those chirping kibitzers, the gophers;
But, by and large, the friends we made
Were in our own hard-bitten legions,
Though snorting freight-trains on the grade
Gave us a glimpse of outer regions.

As weeks went by, I realized
That every man of all our lot—
Magyar, Ukrainian, Pole, or Scot—
Had some deep vision that he prized,
And that behind each one there lay
Some tragic cause that made him stray
Beyond the parish of his birth
To this bleak corner of the earth.

II

As neighbour to my bunk I had
A slender, brown-haired Magyar lad,
Young Imre Szabó, harshly torn
From the far land where he was born
By woes of war and revolution
That brought him down to destitution
And placed some millions of his folk
Under an iron foreign yoke.
He had been born in Transylvania,
At Kolozsvár, among the hills,

But ragged armies of Roumania
Brought to the land a thousand ills,
And both the parents he adored
Were slaughtered by the hostile horde.
He had been trained as a musician
At Kolozsvár and Budapest,
And had secured a good position
At the Liszt College, when the crest
Of revolution reached its height
And killed his prospects over-night.
Hence, of all work and wealth bereft
In the sad country of his kin,
After some hungry months he left
Another chapter to begin
With indescribable emotion
In western lands beyond the ocean.
But even here no work was found
For a superb first violinist.
The theatres used films for sound,
And so his living was the thinnest,
Until by quick degrees he came
To join the rough construction game
And warp his fine artistic hand
In lugging ties and tamping sand.
One warm, deep passion moved his life—
Love for a girl, his blue-eyed Sári,
Whom he proposed to make his wife;
And she as well seemed keen to marry

As soon as he, by eager toil,
Could bring her to Canadian soil.
Thus, as by day he worked near me
In trousers of old dungaree,
With knotted rope-strands for a belt,
And somehow smiled, I knew he felt
That all this hardship, though severe,
Would bring his Sári yet more near.
Or when at evening he would lie
Upon his bunk, and smile, and sigh,
I knew his thoughts were far away
Envisioning a happier day.
In time, he told me all his hope
And all the story of his past;
And though the young lad did not mope
About those days that could not last,
Yet memories were his existence
And his poor soul found its subsistence
In recollections sweet and far
Of summer nights in Kolozsvár
When the acacias were in bloom
And through the tender twilight gloom
The babbling Szamos whispered low
To the two lovers wandering slow,
Till starlight touched their happy cheeks
Beneath the Transylvanian peaks.
Or he recalled, beyond the rest,
One magic night in Budapest,

When high upon the Gellért heights
They sat and watched the myriad lights
In jewelled radiance illumine
The city like a sleeping woman.
Far down, the Danube eddied fleet
Dark, velvet waters at their feet,
And gypsy music floated still
Across the silence of the hill,
Stirring the heart in poignant fashion
With deathless hope and hopeless passion.
He was to seek, at dawn of day,
Another country far away
Beyond the salt, soul-sundering sea,
That there, with thrift and energy,
He might create an Eden fair
And bring his blue-eyed sweetheart there.
And so that night in Budapest
Before he sought an alien West,
They sat and talked the whole night through,
And kissed and cried, as lovers do,
And vowed that though harsh fate might sever
Their paths awhile, yet, blocked by none,
Their faithful love would last forever,
While hills should stand and rivers run.
With such remembrances enshrined
Imperishably in his mind,
He bore harsh toil and pain and ache,
And deemed it light for Sári's sake.

III

One August day, a letter came,
A cold, brief message from her mother,
To say, without a word of blame,
That Sári had espoused another.
Had she been there, and I had heard her,
I would have told her it was murder;
For Imre never smiled again
In that rough world of working men,
And it was plain, with no word spoken,
The mainspring of his life was broken.
The end came soon. For when, that fall,
An onset of pneumonia faced him,
He did not fight the thing at all,
And six days later we had placed him
In a low grave of prairie clay
Along the lonely right of way.

Few of our people realize
How countless railway tracks and ties
Are laid with human blood and sweat,
And those who know it, soon forget,
While all the voiceless, toiling lot—
Magyar, Ukrainian, Pole, and Scot—
Go each their humble, tragic ways
After the rough construction days.
As for the many who remain

Beneath the grasses of the plain,
Like that young lad of dreams and sighs,
Only the coyotes' mournful cries
As dusk comes on, express to me
The sense of all their tragedy."

THE PRIEST'S TALE

of

THE RED RIVER TRAGEDY

PROLOGUE

Farthest of any from the fire
Of all who yarned and puffed in peace
Was an old priest who smoked a briar,
A Manitoba-born *Métis*
Whose heart had never wished to sally
Beyond the old Red River Valley.
"In blends of Indian and white,"
Exclaimed the lawyer, "I am sure
The Indian seems to pass from sight;
At least the type is never pure.
I doubt if the authentic strain
E'er comes in spirit back again."
The old priest murmured contradiction:
"I have a story from my youth,
And though it sounds like wildest fiction
I can assure you it is truth,
For with my boyhood eyes I saw
A man revert and be as raw
And fierce a savage, past restraint,
As ever fought in battle-paint."

We held our peace; we did not fear
A feeble tale from such as he.
And so we heard with eager ear
An old Red River tragedy:

THE PRIEST'S TALE

I

THE dark Red River never pauses
In moving on its northward course,
Inscrutable as primal causes
And as relentless in its force;
Through level leagues of plain it passes,
Across a green infinitude
Of springing grain and prairie grasses,
In endless progress, still renewed,
Past Aubigny and Letellier,
St. Jean Baptiste and Ste. Agathe,
White St. Adolphe and white Cartier,
Where, by the River and the flat,
Frenchman and Cree, in mingled strains,
Are domiciled upon the plains.
Centuries since, before the French
Had mated with their dusky daughters,
The Red Men had been wont to drench
Deep in the River's turbid waters

A yearly human sacrifice
To the grim spirit of the flood,
Who would be friendly at the price
Of duly offered human blood.
  Led by the shaman, one spring day,
They would assemble on the shore,
Standing in ranks upon the clay,
And while the sorcerer went before
Through all his holy rites and charms,
Would copy, as in mute kotow,
His solemn flexures of the arms
And three times beaten breast and brow
As silent prelude to the death
Of one who still drew living breath.
But who, when marked by the magician,
Died freely, of his own volition.
  An Indian teepee-village stood
Just at the present Aubigny,
And there, beside a little wood,
The sacrifice was wont to be—
A solemn service to placate
A Spirit capable of hate.
No other spot that Red Men knew
Commanded equal reverence
Except the Straits of Manitou,
On His great lake, where confluence
Of flooding waves dread sounds awoke
As if the Chief of Spirits spoke.

But ever since bold French begot
On Indian wives a mingled race,
Their sons, as Christians, have forgot
The ancient horror of the place,
Save as an undertone of feeling
Scarce realized or worth concealing.
The steepled church beside the Stream
Lifts its triumphant cross on high;
No pious villager would dream
That he could flout it, or deny;
And yet in this small town befell
The startling story that I tell.

II

When I was but a little boy,
The prettiest lass in Aubigny
And fittest for some lover's joy
Was Paul Couture's big girl Marie.
She was as supple as a willow;
Her hair was black, her lips were red;
Her budding bosom was a pillow
On which a king might lay his head;
Her voice was like a quiet brook;
Modest she was from head to feet;
And every man would turn to look
When she went shyly down the street.

Two men were rivals for her love:
Adolphe Dufresne and Jacques Bazin,
Each of them well equipped to prove
Her model of a fine young man.
Jacques was a trifle under size,
With beetling brows and brooding eyes,
But he was handsome in his way,
Lithe as a panther when he walked,
And a great 'cello seemed to play
Deep in his throat whene'er he talked,
Voicing, for anyone to sense,
A nature tender and intense.
But young Adolphe was tall and straight,
With Scipionic brow and nose,
Born to command, in love or hate,
Imperious even in repose,
And his clear voice would mount and soar
Like trumpets summoning to war.
Both men were French in name and training;
Both to the holy Faith held fast;
Yet in their features, without straining,
One saw, four generations past,
How Indian fire and arrogance
Had mingled with the blood of France.

Howe'er Marie made up her mind,
Make it she did: and it was clear
That with the months her heart inclined
To hold Adolphe as much more dear.

But Jacques Bazin grew pale with moping;
Ever he racked his tortured brain,
Through labyrinths of passion groping
For some dark answer to his pain.
  I was a boy, as I have said,—
A little, black-haired lad of nine;
And even yet I thrill with dread
In thinking what a sight was mine
One day in spring, with knees a-shiver,
Hid in a thicket by the River.

III

I had been playing in that wood
Where shamans long ago had stood,
When, at a sudden voice, I shrank
Among the hazels by the bank,
And, peering through them fearfully,
I saw Adolphe and his Marie
Stand side by side; in threatening fashion
Jacques faced them in a towering passion.
Short breaths his heaving breast expelled,
And in his twitching hands he held
A one-barrel shot-gun, half-uplifted;
Then, with an oath, the gun was shifted
Up to his shoulder, thus to cover
The heart of the successful lover.
'Ah, mon Dieu, non!' cried out Marie,
And flung herself upon the breast

Of her Adolphe with loyalty
Just as Jacques' trigger-finger pressed
And the gun gave a murderous roar
That echoed on from shore to shore.
Thus, as her fragrant body clung
One quivering moment to her lover,
Black buckshot tore through back and lung
A wound whence no one could recover.
Blood spurted. With convulsive moan
She kissed him, and her soul had flown.
  Adolphe stood staring one brief space,
Then laid the warm, dear corpse aside,
And in pale fury turned to face
Him who had robbed him of a bride.
Jacques used his spent gun as a club;
Adolphe had but a pocket-knife,
But would have slain Beelzebub
In that grim fight of death and life.
For though again and yet again
Jacques' blows broke ribs and collar-bone,
He seemed impervious to pain,
And, stabbing fiercely, claimed his own
In streaming wounds on face and throat
Till Jacques grew feebler as he smote
And sank at last upon the clay,
Gasping his frenzied life away.
Then his foe helped the soul depart
With savage knife-thrusts through the heart,

And, in a weirder spectacle,
Grappling the hair of him now dead,
He drew the knife-blade round the skull
And wrenched the scalp from off the head.
Erect he stood then, French no more
But purest savage, scalp in hand.
All dabbled with his foeman's gore,
Upon the corpse I saw him stand
And raise with shrill intensity
The war-whoop of the ancient Cree!

IV

As when dark clouds, as night draws on,
Succeed a lurid sunset-flame,
A bleaker, sadder mood anon
Over the suffering lover came.
Dropping the scalp with sudden loathing,
He turned with tears to his Marie,
Patted her hair and smoothed her clothing,
And took her gently on his knee.
Then, as I watched him from my thicket,
I saw how yet another mood
Entered his grieving mind, to prick it
Out of its tearful lassitude.
It was a mood as primitive
And pagan as his scalping-fit:
All of the years that I may live
I shall recall the thrill of it.

Lifting her body up, he strode
A few short steps and seemed to greet
The deep Red River's waves that flowed,
A turbid torrent, at his feet.
As in a trance, he laid her down
And faced the River, grim and brown.
He wove before it gestured charms—
No Sign of Cross to seal a vow,
But solemn flexures of the arms
And three times beaten breast and brow
As if in prelude to the death
Of one who still drew living breath.
Then, with Marie in his embrace,
He cast himself without a quiver,
But rather with a Stoic grace,
Deep in the eddies of the River.

V

Near Ste. Agathe, some two weeks later,
The bodies, side by side, were found;
And but for me, the sole spectator,
A place in consecrated ground
Had been forbidden to a man
Whose suicide seemed plain to scan.
But I, the only witness, swore
That as he staggered, well nigh spent,
To bear her home along the shore,
He'd tumbled in by accident.

And so, still dubious and loath,
In one green plot they buried both.
But if my falsehood was a sin
And God is vexed to have him in,
I know that with efficient plea
Her soul will intercede for me
As well as him for whom she died
In springtime, by the River's side—
That broad Red River, dark, sublime,
That, on these prairies, seems to me
Our turbid human stream of Time
Through prairies of Eternity."

The Parson's Tale *of* THE GIMLI PRODIGAL

PROLOGUE

We watched the hearth-fire for a time
In silence. Then the drover said:
"I wonder if a youth of crime
Has ever turned to good instead?"—
"Sometimes it has," the parson ventured.
"Sometimes a lad to hell indentured
Has proved a hero, fit for glory.
Yes, I am thinking of a story."—
"Go on," we urged him. "Tell your tale."—
"Granted," he answered. "That I shall."
And so he traced for us the trail
Of the young Gimli prodigal.

THE PARSON'S TALE

I

THERE was a youth," he started primly,
"Whose habitation was in Gimli,
That bleak Icelandic fishing-village
From which the boats go out to pillage
The waters of Lake Winnipeg.
He was a badly addled egg:

For when you questioned anyone
About young Olaf Helgason,
A sadly shaken head would mourn
The utter shipwreck of his days,
And mothers used his name to warn
Their children from ungodly ways.
He was good-looking, tall and fair,
Blue-eyed, with Scandinavian hair,
And with that Irish nose, perforce,
That marks his nation from the Norse;
Yet all his gifts of form and face
Served but to heighten his disgrace.
His boyhood had been strict and stern;
His father, Helgi, as I learn,
Had been the grimmest, soberest liver
From Selkirk north to Berens River.
But when the old man's fishing-yawl
Was lost in a September squall,
Paternal thrift bequeathed the boy
A tidy fortune to enjoy.
Scorning his widowed mother's pleas,
He plunged into a gulf of ease
And grew expert to guzzle rum
With swinish males and female scum
In dark resorts of evil fame,
Dishonouring an honoured name.
But when these rats had picked him clean
Of all his little patrimony,

They coached the wild young wolverine
In devious ways to catch a coney;
Yet though he tried all forms of swindling
His hopes to side-step work kept dwindling,
Till desperation led in time
To fiercer, bolder forms of crime.
One night, with 'Slimy' Popovitch,
Who also had a thievish itch,
He paid a well-armed midnight call
On Gimli's Bank of Montreal,
Made entry, and began assault
Upon the safe within the vault.
The golden crib was well-nigh cracked
When Mounties caught them in the act.
'Put up your hands!' a red-coat said.
'What are you doing here, you bummers?'—
'Lay off!' says Olaf, turning red.
'We're just a helpful pair of plumbers.'—
'Then come with me,' the Mountie lours
'For working after union hours!'
Since Olaf had an automatic
Ready for action on his hip,
The magistrate was most emphatic
In giving him a five-year trip;
And so he settled the account in
A steel-barred cell at Stony Mountain.

II

A sadder and a wiser man,
Young Olaf was turned loose at last,
Telling the Warden that his plan
Was bravely to live down his past
Back in the little fishing-port
Where he had been condemned in court.
His white-haired mother welcomed him
With faltering step and eyes grown dim,
But the community at large
Was hostile over his discharge:
'This mouldy jail-bird from the Pen,'
They said in scorn, 'Should go on west,
And not compete with decent men
Where once he fouled an honest nest.
Why should he hope to find a job
Here, where he loafed, a thieving snob?'
In vain for weeks he looked about,
Till Walter Kvaran, full of pity
For the old mother, tried him out
In gutting gold-eyes for the City.
It was a job that stank supremely,
A bilious task and hard to stomach,
But he endured the stench unseemly,
The dripping knife, the reeking hummock
Of fishy offal and the rest,
Because he dared not fail the test.

Under the summer sun he toiled.
Though blistering dog-days almost broiled
The fish on which he plied his blade;
And still all Gimli, man and maid
Looked with suspicion on the lad,
Regarding him as wholly bad.
  August the Second duly came,
And an Icelandic celebration
Was held at Hnausa in the name
Of their renowned ancestral nation.
Thither in zest came everyone
From Arborg and from Riverton
And all the coast-folk, near and far,
From Gimli up to Sandy Bar.
Then children of the Arctic Isle
Upheld their old inheritance:
Some wrestled in Icelandic style,
And some led out the Viking dance,
And there were poets, old and young,
Grey Stephan G. and Guttormur—
Iceland and Canada were sung
In odes that made the heart-strings stir.
But to young Olaf one fair scene
Caused every other view to fade—
It was the crowning of the Queen,
The white *Fjallkona*, 'Mountain-maid':
For Sigrun, Gimli's fairest lass,
His school-mate in a day gone by,

Was deemed that season to surpass
All others for this honour high.
Serene and lovely, tall and sweet,
She sat upon her Viking throne—
A simple girl at whose shy feet
The tribute of a day was shewn.
Her eyes the glance of Olaf crossed:
He looked, and loved her, and was lost.
That night with hopeless, throbbing head
He lay upon his humble bed:
For how could he, who toiled in squalor
Under the shadow of a crime
And needed every hard-won dollar
To help his mother, hope in time
That she, the fairest queen of all,
Might wed the Gimli prodigal?
He knew, moreover, that his boss,
Big Walter Kvaran, whose good heart
Had saved his life from utter loss,
Had sought to play the lover's part,
And that, unless all plans miscarried,
Another year would see them married.
Walter was forty, to be sure,
A widower and plain of face,
But he was rich, his life was pure,
His name unspotted by disgrace.
Olaf had noted with surprise
A kindly light in Sigrun's eyes,

And yet he felt his hopes were barren
Compared with those of Walter Kvaran.
  Day after day, amid his toil,
Her peerless face possessed his mind.
The foulest labour could not soil
A week in which her glance was kind.
And yet he held himself aloof,
Fearing the scorn of swift reproof,
And sought to mitigate the curse
Of hopeless love by setting down
In measures of Icelandic verse
The passion that he could not drown:

'Sigrun only do I sigh for,
Sadly moan my low estate.
Sick and lone, true life I cry for.
Love atones my evil fate!'

Such were the ring-rhymes that he fashioned
After the rules of ancient metre,
Feeling their permanence impassioned
Must somehow make his love completer.
But still he kept his verses hid
And breathed to no one what he did.

III

Hard frosts came early that November,
Rimming the shores with shining ice.
Few of the settlers could remember

A colder fall. And since the price
Of fish was high and times were hard,
No fear the fishermen debarred,
After the coastal waters froze,
From netting whitefish through the floes.
Foremost among them, Walter sought
With three bold men to take his store;
And every night on sleds they brought
A silvery harvest to the shore.
And there, the scaly bellies ripping,
Salted the fish for early shipping.
  One Friday, when the morning broke,
A heavy east wind rose and blew
Out of a sky of leaden hue
And to tumultuous life awoke
The twenty miles of open water
Beyond the ice-floes. But the slaughter
Of precious whitefish did not cease,
Although beneath the gleaming floes
A heaving ground-swell's strength arose
And groaned, and gave the ice no peace,
Cracking it clean in many a spot
With uproar like a cannon-shot.
At two o'clock, the east wind fell.
At half past four, a wild north-wester
Swooped, like a blizzard loosed from hell,
As if relentless to sequester

Some hapless fragment of the floe
And drive it to the open lake—
Nor swooped in vain. With movement slow,
Under its impulse, a great cake
Broke from its mooring near the shore
And on it, unsuspecting, bore
Big Walter Kvaran and the three
Who shared his daily industry.
Too late they startled and looked back
And saw between them and the land
A lane of water wide and black,
And frantic watched that lane expand:
No voice could pierce that snow-filled gale;
They waved their arms to speak their plight;
But every effort seemed to fail
Across the deepening dusk of night.
Dimmer and farther grew the town.
With lamplit windows in the gloom.
Ever more certain seemed their doom
As ever mightier waves bore down
And battered fragments from the floe;
They knew they had not far to go
Before their ice-isle would be tossed
To nothing and be wholly lost.
Then, on the waves, they seemed to mark
A blacker black within the dark.

IV

It was a boat, with Olaf in it,
Tossing upon the icy waves.
Now some great billow seems to spin it,
And now once more the skiff behaves
As if in dogged bravery
It sought their rescuer to be.

In Gimli, when the blizzard broke,
Olaf was in the packing-sheds,
Intent on shovelling whitefish-heads
Into the refuse-vat. Then spoke
A frantic voice beside his ear:
It was old Hrefna Helgason,
His mother, who beyond the pier
Had marked the drifting ice-floe run
Into the heaving, storm-lashed lake
With the four men, and for their sake
Had rushed to gasp the message out
In Walter's fish-sheds. With a shout,
Olaf ran quickly to the beach
And gazed across the gathering night
To where, a mile beyond their reach,
The fated four had passed from sight.
Others soon gathered by him there
And spoke in counsels of despair:
'The schooners are laid up for winter.'
'Walt's rowboat is the only thing.'—

'In storm and floe that boat might splinter;
And it's so small one man would fling
His life to chance in rescuing four.
That boat takes five and not one more.'—
'A man were mad to risk that fate!'—
'Who'll go?'—'Not I! It's now too late.'

Olaf stood silent as they talked;
Swift thought made tumult in his brain:
Walter was gone, the man who baulked
His love for Sigrun. Not in vain
Hereafter might his wooing prove.
He might aspire to Sigrun's charms.
Already, in a dream of love,
He held her warm within his arms;
And riches too in fancy came
To add their glamour to his name.

Then out of unguessed deeps of thought
A starker, sterner mood arose—
A man's strong purpose, making taut
His muscles, while his young face froze
To icy resolution. Surely
Out of his far Icelandic past
Heroic impulse now beat purely
To argue him a man at last.
His father, Helgi, once had taught him
His lineage of a thousand years;
And now, perhaps, remembrance caught him,
Perhaps that roll-call filled his ears—

Helgi and Axel, Sveinn and Bjarni,
Gisli and Kolbeinn, Páll and Gest,
Snorri and Sigurbjörn and Arni,
Gunnar and Oddur and the rest—
And in his heart he heard them speaking,
Those generations in his blood;
Dim in his mind he saw them seeking
Greatly their sea-borne livelihood.
Along that misty Arctic island
He saw their fishing-vessels tossed;
By skerry, reef, and craggy highland,
Their lives, but not their souls, were lost.
Thus, as he stood there in his place,
He quenched all thought of love or pelf,
Uplifted on a tide of race
That made him greater than himself.

Into the lake he rowed alone,
Into the darkness and the storm,
Until at last the boat's frail form
Was lost to sight, and with a moan
Old Hrefna sank upon the snow,
Unable to conceal her woe.

Thus, in their need, the four lost men,
Their garments stiff with icy scurf,
Beheld him sweep into their ken,
Seeking their floe across the surf.
They cheered; then felt their joy withdraw
And turn to horror, as they saw

The skiff against the floe capsize
And Olaf sink before their eyes,
Never to reappear. In vain
They sought him, and at last in pain
They turned the boat's prow to the shore
And with two men on either oar
Into the storm they battled grimly
Over the billows back to Gimli. . . .

There's really not much more to tell.
Walter was laid up for a spell . . .
Pneumonia . . . And Hrefna found
The songs to Sigrun, and went round
And called on Sigrun with a view
To finding whether Sigrun knew
Olaf had loved her, and the price
And measure of his sacrifice.
Whether she did, I can't unfold;
For neither woman ever told.
But when in time she wed with Walter
And a male baby duly came,
She knew her mind, and did not alter
Her choice of Olaf as his name.
And in the Gimli graveyard, where
Drowned Olaf by drowned Helgi sleeps,
Through thirty years her tender care
A quiet vigil often keeps."

The parson ceased. A silence fell.
Then said the lawyer: "It appears
That story lives on mighty well
In detail, after thirty years."—
The answer came back, soft and slow:
"With me, his memory is not barren,
Though born but thirty years ago.
My name, you see, is Olaf Kvaran."

THE SECOND FARMER'S TALE
of
THE JOBLESS GAOLBIRD

PROLOGUE

The second farmer's past was Norse.
He was a thoughtful sort of chap,
Fair-haired, as husky as a horse,
And a fine backer in a scrap.
'I like the West,' he said. 'It's true
I'm a Canadian through and through,
And yet it is a grief to me
That with the country's boundless wealth
We have so failed to guarantee
The welfare, happiness, and health
Of every growing lass and lad,
But often send them to the bad
Through lack of work and lack of care
Until they crack in sheer despair.
Even our houses of correction,
Which ought to save them for their time,
Are sometimes centres of infection
And doom the young to lives of crime."
"I scent a story," Casey said.
"Go on, and tell it, without fail!"
And so he willingly complied,
And told a tragic penal tale:

THE SECOND FARMER'S TALE

I

WHEN I was young, I was a guard
Out in the Gaol at Headingly.
The duties were not very hard
For a big husky man like me,
Yet nearly everyone who serves
In such a place develops nerves—
And when I longed to be at large,
I asked, and got, my full discharge.
It's hard to analyse the mood
Of such a place. We liked the food;
And I can give a *bona fide*
I never saw a place more tidy.
But bricks and concrete, brass and steel
Are hard, cold things for men to feel,
And give an atmosphere of gloom
To every cell and cage and room.
Along the concrete floors one's tread
Goes echoing fit to wake the dead,
And steel on steel grates harsh and hard
When keys are turned and bolts are barred.
Yet more depressing still, I think,
Is tending men whose hearts are ink,
The human misfits whom the court
Has banished to this grey resort.

Two types are there, split fifty-fifty:
The one is earnest, kind, and thrifty,
But through weak impulse or bad luck
Has fallen headlong in the muck;
The other lot are bad at heart
And only foul a second start,
Compounding each successive time
The brutal baseness of their crime.
But to a thoughtful man, the worst
Is that the last type and the first
Are mingled here in cell and cage
Without regard for crime or age,
And many a likely lad begins
To learn a sordid list of sins
From vicious lags who never tire
In dragging others in the mire.
Release then means but more offending,
Which all too often has its ending
When in that fatal southwest room
The hangman works his act of doom:
Then, with a clang, the steel trap falls
And echoes through the shuddering halls.

A tragic case that I remember
Was young Jim Tingle from Toronto,
Who rode the rods out one September
Because his work and cash had gone to—
Well, to that hopeless, hungry void
That swallows up the unemployed.

Jim was a winsome sort of boy
With light blue eyes and curly hair,
The sort a father would enjoy
In rearing as his son and heir;
But as an orphan, he was bound
To find his own hard way around.
To make his path more stony still,
The lack of all co-ordination
Between our provinces worked ill
In letting labour, in our nation,
Drift aimlessly from spot to spot
In search of some more active town
Or else in dull stagnation rot
When local industries shut down.
And thus, with many another drifter
Who sought for work and would not beg,
Jim thought of no solution swifter
Than riding freights to Winnipeg.
At first his luck seemed better here,
And for the space of half a year
He worked unloading wholesale meat,
And had a room on Hargrave Street.
In spring, alas, a lay-off came,
And Jim, aged twenty, had no claim
Compared with many a married man
With wife and children's needs to scan.
By summer, all Jim's cash was spent.
His boarding-house, with sundry oaths,

To guarantee arrears of rent,
Then seized his coat and winter clothes.
Hunger grew dire one August day;
And in a mood not felt before,
He tried to smuggle food away
Out of a big department store.
A lynx-eyed clerk was quick to see.
Jim got five months in Headingly.

II

When we first put him under lock,
The lad was dazed with shame and shock.
He had been reared with grace and knowledge,
And had a year or two of college,
When both his parents' deaths had thrown
The youngster wholly on his own.
Week after week, I looked at Jim
And watched the workings of his mind
To see if gaol had curdled him
And turned his soul against his kind.
I saw the old lags at their game
Of urging him to put off shame
And find revenge in hateful glee
In war upon society.
But Jim was made of better stuff—
A day or two before he left
He told me he had had enough:
He'd die before he'd stoop to theft.

When January closed his stay,
The gaol truck took him in to town,
And, with a chilly 'Well, good day!',
Pulled to the curb and let him down,
Dressed only in the summer suit
That he had worn at his arrest,
Of overcoat quite destitute—
No hat, no underwear, no vest,
And in his pocket not a cent
To feed or lodge him where he went!
He sought his former boarding-place,
But Mrs. Gooch, who met his ring,
Just slammed the front door in his face
And vowed he had not left a thing.
He sought his old employers out,
But found the boss refused to see him;
From firm to firm he trudged about,
But none from his distress would free him;
And if he chanced to beg a dime,
They cried that begging was a crime
And threatened him with the police
If the black practice did not cease.
In zero weather, thinly clad,
He shivered on from shop to shop,
A hungry and disheartened lad
Who saw no place where he could stop
There on the icy winter street
Down which the north wind wailed and beat,

Till Hop Lee Ching, whose bedroom lay
Above his little frame café,
Shared food and bed that night with Jim
When every door was barred to him
And all the Christian city stood
As heartless as a winter wood.
Next morning, with a stifled sob,
He started out to find a job;
But all men asked him, without fail,
How he had left his last employ,
And when they heard about the Gaol
They simply would not hire the boy.
To make it short, within a week
Of starting his unheeded plea,
A bobby found him, staggering weak,
And ran him in for vagrancy.

III

This time we got him back defiant.
All the old-timers in his flat
Now found in him a willing client,
And at their wicked feet he sat.
They taught the lad in easy stages
At talking-time along the cages,
And he would learn with bitter zeal
The way that steel can bite on steel
In drilling safes, and what expense
Would fix one's takings with a fence,

What lawyers were the best for crooks,
And how to fake a set of books.
Then he was taught by 'Stinky' Bates,
An old past master at the game,
To pinch a car and change the plates
And file the numbers off the frame.
Then a sleek Russian, Ivan Bunin,
Was always sure to come and tune in,
And urge on him, as his solution,
A glorious time of revolution,
When all the Workers would arise
And make this Continent their prize:
'The turnkey and the Governor,
Would then,' he muttered, 'scrub the floor,
While we, exultant to condemn,
Prepared the hangman's drop for them,
And shot the *boorzhoys,* days and nights,
Through all their homes in River Heights.'
But the most voluble of all
Was an old burglar, 'Butch' McColl,
Alias Brown, Brock, Bryce, and Vales,
A seasoned connoisseur in gaols.
He claimed he'd been in every one
From New Orleans to Edmonton:
'And some were very bad,' he'd say,
'And some were good, and this to-day
Rates on the whole as pretty good
In style and quality of food,

Except that Ivan, the big dope,
Once dosed the soup with laundry soap
To start a riot, for he likes
The raw, red violence of strikes.
I fear that if in time the stars
Bring all his fevered plans to birth,
The Comrades and the Commissars
Will make our life a hell on earth;
For ruthless Red minorities,
With acid in their veins for blood,
Would do with people as they please
And trample freedom in the mud.
Don't listen when his mad dreams fizz!
Just take the country as it is:
And though we sometimes get our lickings,
A clever crook can have his pickings.'
Such were his mentors, week by week;
And when they were released before him,
They gave him an address to seek,
As proof of the good will they bore him—
And when at last he too was free,
He planned a life of burglary.

IV

That very morning he set out
To look for Ivan, Butch, and Bates,
And found the trio just about
To pull a job. 'At equal rates,'

Said Butch, 'come in and work with us!
I think you'll be a useful cuss.
Meet us to-night at half-past-ten.
Here is some cash to last till then.
In the big safe we're going to crack
There's plenty. None of us will lack.'
Then 'Stinky' vowed, with many a nod,
That Jim would have no vain regrets;
And Ivan handed him a rod
And marihuana cigarettes,
Those hashish-fags that fill the mind
With killer's lust against mankind.
That evening, in the streaming rain,
He walked with frenzy in his brain,
Born of the deadly murder-weed
That nerves the heart to any deed.
As luck would have it, the detectives
Had been tipped off to Butch's plot
To crack the safe; and two effectives
Were there in ambush on the spot.
When Jim and the old-timer trio
Had just begun to ply their tools,
The bobbies challenged them *con brio,*
But when, in keeping with all rules,
The old lags ducked and ran away,
Jim with defiance turned to stay
And shoot it out with the police
In murderous mood and mad caprice.

Then, in a swift and fatal start,
His first slug found one bobby's heart.
His second bullet chanced to plough
A crease across the other's brow
And drop him likewise, as if dead,
Although it had but grazed his head.
Jim paused, and gasped, in sudden fright,
And hurried out into the night—
A night less dark, with storm and rain,
Than the black tumult in his brain.

V

With six big prowl-cars on his trail,
A roused police force tracked him down,
And as the dawn was turning pale,
Found him, the sanest man in town,
A pale and penitent offender
And more than ready to surrender.
Out in a gaol-cage once again,
He sat and brooded, in such pain
That Hell could never hope to see
More utter, hopeless misery.
It was too dark, the thing he felt,
For that next night, to find surcease,
He hanged himself with his own belt,
And so, at last, poor Jim had peace,
There in that gloomy concrete den
That altered him, a simple lad,

Into an enemy of men
And slowly changed the good to bad.
  Who killed Jim Tingle? It's my claim
That he himself was not to blame,
But you, and I, and all the rest
Who in this wide, abundant West
With all our wealth have failed to give
Each man a chance to work and live.
To me, the case was most alarming;
And I resigned and took to farming.
Close to the soil, it seems to me,
One faces a reality
In life and labour past compare;
And that is why I'm staying there."

THE TEACHER'S TALE

of

THE DYNAMO KING

PROLOGUE

The grey-haired teacher barked assent.
"It often seems to me," he said,
"That social forces circumvent
The finest men our age has bred,
And that our weakness in the mass
Frustrates those men who, as a class,
Would lead us on to higher things
Beyond our wildest reckonings.
I'm thinking of a splendid chap
Who might have helped to change our time
Had not a tragical mishap
Destroyed him in his early prime."
"I think I know the man you mean,"
The lawyer said. "A good man gone!
But do not let me intervene."
And so the teacher thus went on:

THE TEACHER'S TALE

I

THE brightest boy I ever taught
Was little Axel Pavlidek,
Into whose fabric fate had wrought
A fruitful blend of Swede and Czech.
His father had been born in Prague,
And studied law at Lund and Leyden.
A Swedish woman at the Hague
Became his wife and helped to widen
The great ideals of his soul,
Embracing mankind as a whole.
Their only child, a little boy
Named Axel, was just twelve years old
When they both died, and all his joy
Was by their loss left crushed and cold.
Then, by some whimsy of the law,
An uncle out in Canada
Becomes his guardian; summer passes;
And autumn finds him in my classes
In a red school-house, squat and plain,
A few miles north of Boissevain.
In all my years, I had not seen
A lad so winsome and so keen.
He had the forehead of Apollo,
Thin, wistful lips, and dreamy eyes,

And all the time he seemed to follow
The lessons with a glad surprise
That knowledge, promptly understood,
Could be so simple and so good.
Speaking four other tongues already,
He mastered English in his stride;
And his demands on me were steady
For mathematics far more wide
Than high school systems in the West
Had ever sanctioned at their best.
Binomials might keep the class
In constant sorrows and dejections,
But Axel with a smile would pass
To calculus and conic sections,
And raise the happiest of ructions
With surds, quaternions, and fluxions.
Next year, at University
In Winnipeg, he likewise kept
The best instructors full of glee,
Until at last he lightly swept
All scholarships and medals clean—
An M. Sc. at seventeen.
After securing, like a gale,
A science doctorate at Yale,
He gave the world of deeds a hearing
And shifted into Engineering,
Deeming the highest task of all
A destiny electrical,

A human culture based on power
In earth's supreme and final hour.

II

The stirring age of thirty-five
Found him the foremost in the West
Among all engineers alive
In seeking wholly to invest
Our land with power—to set man free
On tides of electricity.
The busy whirl of dynamos
Made sweetest music in his ear:
In their deep murmur he could hear
The accent of a force that rose
Out of the currents of the earth
To bring a fairer age to birth.
To him the loveliest of sights
Was the refulgent Northern Lights,
Witness to unseen tides that race
Across the tingling gulfs of space
As sun and planets all rehearse
One vast galvanic universe.
The moon-drawn surge was full of strength
That might be harnessed in due time;
Each river would be dammed at length
To make our life on earth sublime;
For he would bind the streams and seas,
Not in presumptuous vanities—

Mere power for the power's sake—
But in his dreams he hoped to make
A world of peace and health and law,
And plenty, mixed with pious awe,
When all to children would be kind
And man would train his noble mind,
Free from the iron chains of toil;
Even earth's hard and niggard soil
Would be enriched in every field
By virtues that the air would yield
Under the fierce electric might
Pulsating on by day and night.
'The ancient Caesars,' he would say,
'In their imperial excess,
Ranked, in their rule of Nature, less
Than any humble home to-day;
Yet ours is but the opening stage
Of a supreme Electric Age.'

In course of time, he got a grant
To build a mighty Hydro plant
Out in the wilderness of spruce,
Where a great river wandered loose,
By leagues of lake and forest fed
And in a rough and craggy tract
Cascading down its granite bed
In cataract on cataract.

Here Axel's project grew apace,
With coffer-dam and bridge and sluice;

Great dynamos were soon in place
And ready for impending use;
While far away, in endless line,
Grey towers of thin aluminum
Borne shining cables, light and fine,
Soon to be vital with the hum
Of that unseen, dynamic fire
That leaps along the living wire.

III

The mighty task was almost finished,
When, with his ardour undiminished,
Young Axel to the city went
By car, to see the Government
About some detail, handled better
In person than by 'phone or letter.
It was an evening in July;
He just had passed the Lower Fort,
South-bound; and saw great cars roar by,
Seeking some northern beach-resort,—
And half the young lads at the wheel
Were full of 'hooch' from head to heel.
Then, at a curve, a racing Nash,
Seeking, insane, to pass the rest,
Hit Axel head-on with a crash
That crushed the ribs in half his chest
And made his little roadster pitch
In crumpled ruin in the ditch,

There to take fire and in disaster
Burn fatally its stricken master.
As for the snivelling, drunken lout
Who brought this ghastly thing about,
He got off clear without a scratch
And even proved in time a match
For the stern courts, that can be licked
When coward juries won't convict."

The Poet's Tale

of

THE DARKENING DREAM

PROLOGUE

At last the hour was growing late.
Some talked of bed. Said Casey: "Wait!
This quiet fellow in the corner,
Like well-known Master Jackie Horner,
Has had his finger in the pie
By way of listening, but is shy
In speaking out, for he alone
Has told no story of his own."
Then with a smile he turned to me.
"Round off the evening, Sir!" said he.
"I swear by Joseph's coloured coats,
I've watched you all day taking notes
There in the corner, and I'm sure,
Though you look timid and demure,
You have some stirring tale to tell
Will please our group almighty well."
Confronted thus by his intent,
I wriggled with embarrassment:
"If I were wise, I would decline,
For stories are not in my line;

But lest I seem, with thankless heart,
Unwilling to play out my part,
I shall tell briefly of a dream
From which I wakened with a scream
Only last night. As I'm a sinner,
It was not due to Casey's dinner—
I would not be misunderstood,
For this hotel is mighty good—
But some distemper in my veins
Produced in me these psychic pains.
Whether the vision had a meaning
Some one of you perhaps can tell.
I only know it had a leaning
Towards agonizing pangs of hell."
The rest were silent, so anon
I cleared my throat and thus went on:

THE POET'S TALE

I

I DREAMT I saw a marshy plain,
A scummy waste of stagnant rain,
And from it, like a sloping roof,
An eastward hillside drew aloof.
Up that broad mountain, countless men,
Emerging from the dismal fen,
Walked bravely upwards towards the height,

Their brows a-glow with morning light;
For high above the eastern rim,
Brighter than hosts of cherubim,
A blaze of glory had begun,
At times a cross, at times a sun.
Slowly the human army climbed,
With marshy traces still beslimed,
While each was faithful to the other
And helped him upward like a brother.
It was a soul-inspiring sight
To see kind faces gleaming bright
And see reflected in each eye
The holy glory in the sky.

After long ages, as it seemed,
It was a darker thing I dreamed.
For some no longer faced the sun,
But from earth's iron entrails spun
Fantastic types of cold machine
Such as mankind had never seen—
Machines for sport and recreation,
For government, and education,
To heal man's body and restore him,
And do his very thinking for him.
And as man's trust, through such abettal,
Was less on faith and more on metal,
The radiant light of heaven grew dim
And earth seemed merciless and grim.

II

I saw my dream grow darker yet,
And all the heavens overset
With a miasmic fog of night
That choked and hid the earlier light.
Across the land, in horrid zeal,
Crawled giant dinosaurs of steel,
Churning the hillside into mire
And belching lead and gouts of fire.
Before them maddened thousands fled,
And thousands in their path lay dead.
From lairs of concrete in the hills
Slid pterodactyls, broad of wing,
With leaden murder in their bills
And in their throats loud muttering,
Demanding horror in a flood
And mighty draughts of human blood.
With hideous roars they swept the skies
Or ranged the fields like monstrous flies;
And those who fled the dinosaurs
These flying creatures killed by scores.
Some remnants of the race of man
Then down the slope in frenzy ran,
And after them steel monsters came
With gullets belching smoke and flame,
Driving them, furious and harsh,
To stifle in the ancient marsh.

Just as they sank beneath the scum
And I stood gaping, crazed and dumb,
A pterodactyl swooped at me,
And I awoke in agony . . . "

. . . . .

After an interval of quiet,
Said Casey, "Such a dream of doom
Is no reflection on the diet
I serve you in my dining-room.
Nor has it meaning. That is flat.
In such things, I'm perfect sceptic.
To have a nightmare such as that,
You must have been a born dyspeptic."
The teacher grinned: "Your dream was all
Quite paleontological
And might provide a 'horror classic'
With setting in the Mid-Jurassic.
If dreams like that are writ in stone,
I'd leave Geology alone.
I fancy that your recent reading
Has had a hand in nightmare-breeding."
But the old priest, his hand half-shaking
Said slowly, with a sigh or two:
"My guess is, that he dreamed it waking,
And that its trend is all too true."